700 Common-word Reading and Dictation Exercises

Pitman 2000 Shorthand Edition

700 Common-word Reading and Dictation Exercises

Pitman 2000 Shorthand Edition

The 700 most frequently recurring shorthand outlines with specially selected derivatives, followed by reading and dictation exercises using the outlines listed

Isaac Pitman

PITMAN

PITMAN PUBLISHING LIMITED
39 Parker Street, London WC2B 5PB

Associated Companies
Copp Clark Pitman, Toronto
Fearon Pitman Publishers Inc, San Francisco
Pitman Publishing New Zealand Ltd, Wellington
Pitman Publishing Pty Ltd, Melbourne

Text set in 11 pt Photon Times,
printed by photolithography and bound in Great Britain
at The Pitman Press, Bath

ISBN 0 273 01255 X

G9 (2030:26)

INTRODUCTION

By Sir James Pitman, K.B.E.

The continued success of the New Era edition of 700 Common-word Reading and Dictation Exercises seems to show that the shorthand student and the shorthand teacher have accepted not only willingly but avidly the various principles which underlie the use of the 700 Common Words as a valuable medium for learning shorthand and also for teaching it. A great deal of credit is due to the shorthand teacher and to the student for appreciating these merits, since they do not lie on the surface—in fact the ideas are somewhat revolutionary.

As a result of classroom experience with the 700 Common Words it has been confirmed over and over again that—

1. The 700 Common Words are within the English vocabulary of students; they are the "lowest common language factor."

2. The 700 Common Words recur with 80 per cent frequency in all continuous English: the figures for various examinations of the Royal Society of Arts and of the London Chamber of Commerce without any attempt at selection are as follows—

L.C.C.			R.S.A.		
50 w.p.m.	91·2	per cent	50 w.p.m.	80·8	per cent
60 w.p.m.	87	per cent	60 w.p.m.	81	per cent
70 w.p.m.	91·4	per cent	80 w.p.m.	86·5	per cent
80 w.p.m.	90·7	per cent		83·75	per cent
100 w.p.m.	90	per cent	100 w.p.m.	84·75	per cent
110 110 w.p.m.	82	per cent		85	per cent
			120 w.p.m.	84·6	per cent
120 w.p.m.	82·7	per cent		84·8	per cent
	75·2	per cent	140 w.p.m.	84·3	per cent
130 w.p.m.	85·4	per cent		84·3	per cent
	76·3	per cent	150 w.p.m.	87·5	per cent
150 w.p.m.	80·5	per cent	160 w.p.m.	87	per cent
	80·8	per cent			

These words are therefore in themselves overwhelmingly important for learning and teaching purposes and for use in reading and writing shorthand.

3. Continuous English of an interesting and educative nature on a wide range of subjects can be written within the vocabulary—thanks to the policy in the selection of words useful for meaning. The articles in this book, and many more which have appeared in the two monthly magazines *Memo* and *2000*, are sufficient proof of the capacity of the vocabulary—and are a great tribute to Miss Emily D. Smith, who has followed her great success as a shorthand writer with similar success in this field. The words are therefore the background for the educational value of shorthand.

4. The 700 Common Words are so sufficiently a complete cross-section or sample of English syllables or speech sounds that it is true to say that a knowledge of the principles of the system which is gained from writing the 700 Common Words and the skill with the pen in forming the signs for those syllables have a very close, if not direct, bearing on a knowledge of *all* the rules, and on penmanship ability in *all* other words of the English language. If we examine the words which are not within the 700 Common Words, we find that the great majority of them are formed of syllables within the 700 Common Words, and therefore a mastery of the 700 Common Words, gives a knowledge of rules and penmanship which can be applied in the writing of the other words outside that vocabulary.

This Pitman 2000 Shorthand edition is therefore confidently recommended to teachers, and, above all, to students. The articles provide a means of developing skill in the important words of the language and also (if the contention in No. 4 above is granted) in the material from which almost all other English words are made up. The student should possess a copy of the book and use it for developing his individual skill.

(*a*) First of all, there is the skill of reading. These articles are written with only that very elementary phrasing which is set out in *First Course* and on pages 24–6, and no student should rest content until he can read *every* article fluently.

(*b*) Next there is the skill of penmanship. No student should be satisfied until he can make a perfect copy in a good style of shorthand, writing at a speed of at least 80 words a minute. A perfect copy must have good style, and good style is present only when outlines are written naturally rather than "drawn."

(*c*) Finally, there is the skill in writing from dictation. A student should certainly not be satisfied until he or she can write every one of these articles from dictation at a speed of over 120 words a minute. Any errors in outline or faults in style should be corrected and the remedial skills practised.

Repeated dictation practice from these articles is most valuable to all students, even to those who are seeking high speeds. Only when the pen can automatically form the outlines for these common words will the shorthand writer have release of his other faculties for the task of listening to and hearing one set of words while the pen is forming another set of words.

This parallel text to the New Era edition is invaluable in mixed classes of Pitman 2000 and New Era shorthand writers. Neither group will have any difficulty in reading the shorthand.

Teachers should not hesitate to dictate the same passage a second, third, and more times. A student may think that the English has become familiar. In point of fact, it has, but this fact is of little or no significance. His increase of speed at each repetition is due not to the fact that he knows the English of the passage, but to the fact that he knows what shorthand outline to write when he gets the stimulus of the spoken word, and repetition of stimulus and correct reaction is the basis of skill development.

Students should save the time of their teachers by correcting their dictation notes from their own copy of the book. A high standard of penmanship should be maintained by insisting that students should read back their notes, not on the day on which they are taken but after a considerable lapse of time. Teachers who have an overhead projector and the time to use it will find that a weekly exercise in exhibiting the "cold" shorthand notes of each member of the class in turn, and in class reading from the notes and class criticism of style and of errors, will have a wonderful effect on the standard of penmanship and of shorthand of the whole class.

There are many words in English which are capable of more than one pronunciation and, as Pitman's Shorthand is phonetic, the outline may therefore take more than one form. In cases such as "either" ("iether" and "eether"), "neither" ("niether" and "neether"), "issue" ("isue" and "ishue"), two distinct forms are accepted in the best circles. In North America "eether," "neether" and "ishue" are standard speech and standard Pitman's Shorthand, while in the British Isles the alternative forms "iether," "niether" and "isue" are standard practice.

Modern educators have become more and more convinced that a *real* knowledge of the meaning of words is an essential for progress in any branch of knowledge and so of education itself.

Equally that repetition in the reception and the emission of words in context is a valuable exercise in diminishing any passivity by "skipping" some of the words and thus debasing the value of language as a means of communication.

Students should be encouraged to note—and to confess at any rate to themselves—any word which is thus repeated of which they have doubt as to its meaning *in that context*.

There is nothing more valuable to a shorthand student—or any other—than reference to a good English dictionary. It will be a cause of surprise to learn how many different meanings, in different contexts, a single word may have. Look up in your dictionary the word "set" and understand why it figures in the *Guinness Book of Records* as "the most over-worked word in English which has 58 noun uses, 126 verbal uses and 10 as a participial adjective". I know this because it was I who got it so included.

CONTENTS

Introduction   *Page v*

List of 700 Common Pitman 2000 Shorthand Outlines
arranged in Alphabetical Order   1

Phrases   24

Exercises		Key	Exercises		Key
No.	*Page*	*Page*	*No.*	*Page*	*Page*
1	27	119	21	73	151
2	29	120	22	75	152
3	32	122	23	77	154
4	34	124	24	80	156
5	36	125	25	82	157
6	39	127	26	85	159
7	41	128	27	87	161
8	44	130	28	89	162
9	46	132	29	92	164
10	49	133	30	94	165
11	51	135	31	96	167
12	53	137	32	98	168
13	55	138	33	100	169
14	57	140	34	102	171
15	59	141	35	104	172
16	62	143	36	106	174
17	64	144	37	108	175
18	66	146	38	110	177
19	69	148	39	113	178
20	71	149	40	115	180

LIST OF 700 COMMON PITMAN 2000 SHORTHAND OUTLINES ARRANGED IN ALPHABETICAL ORDER

THESE OUTLINES REPRESENT APPROXIMATELY 68 PER CENT OF THE
WORDS CONTAINED IN ORDINARY ENGLISH MATTER*

A	ANNOUNCE	BED
ABLE	ANOTHER	BEFORE
ABOUT	ANSWER	BEGIN
ABOVE	ANY	BEHIND
ACCORDING	APPEAR	BELIEF
ACCOUNT	APRIL	BELIEVE
ACROSS	ARE	BEST
ACT	ARM	BETTER
ADD	ART	BETWEEN
ADVANTAGE	AS	BEYOND
ADVERTISE	ASK	BIG
AFTER	AT	BLACK
AFTERNOON	ATTEMPT	BLUE
AGAIN	ATTENTION	BOARD
AGE	AUGUST	BODY
AGO	AUTHORITY	BOOK
AGREE	AWAY	BOTH
AIR	AY	BOUGHT
ALL	BABY	BOY
ALONG	BACK	BRAKE
ALSO	BAD	BREAD
ALTOGETHER	BALANCE	BREAK
AM	BANK	BRING
AMONG	BASE	BROTHER
AMOUNT	BE	BROUGHT
AN	BEAUTIFUL	BUILD
AND	BECAUSE	BUILT
ANIMAL	BECOME	BUOY

* See note regarding frequency with derivative outlines, page 8.

1

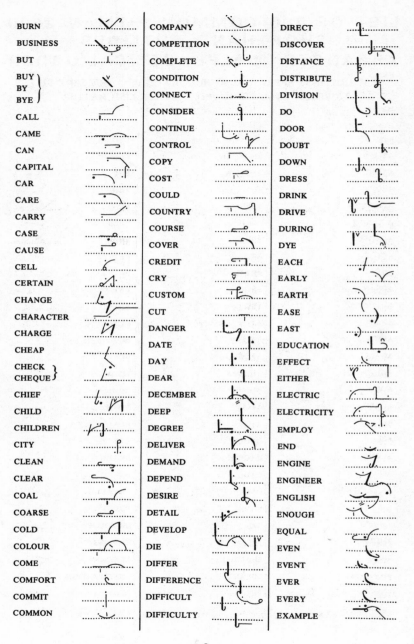

BURN	COMPANY	DIRECT
BUSINESS	COMPETITION	DISCOVER
BUT	COMPLETE	DISTANCE
BUY / BY / BYE	CONDITION	DISTRIBUTE
	CONNECT	DIVISION
CALL	CONSIDER	DO
CAME	CONTINUE	DOOR
CAN	CONTROL	DOUBT
CAPITAL	COPY	DOWN
CAR	COST	DRESS
CARE	COULD	DRINK
CARRY	COUNTRY	DRIVE
CASE	COURSE	DURING
CAUSE	COVER	DYE
CELL	CREDIT	EACH
CERTAIN	CRY	EARLY
CHANGE	CUSTOM	EARTH
CHARACTER	CUT	EASE
CHARGE	DANGER	EAST
CHEAP	DATE	EDUCATION
CHECK / CHEQUE	DAY	EFFECT
CHIEF	DEAR	EITHER
CHILD	DECEMBER	ELECTRIC
CHILDREN	DEEP	ELECTRICITY
CITY	DEGREE	EMPLOY
CLEAN	DELIVER	END
CLEAR	DEMAND	ENGINE
COAL	DEPEND	ENGINEER
COARSE	DESIRE	ENGLISH
COLD	DETAIL	ENOUGH
COLOUR	DEVELOP	EQUAL
COME	DIE	EVEN
COMFORT	DIFFER	EVENT
COMMIT	DIFFERENCE	EVER
COMMON	DIFFICULT	EVERY
	DIFFICULTY	EXAMPLE

2

EXCEPT		FRIDAY		HEAVY	
EXCHANGE		FRIEND		HEIR	
EXIST		FROM		HELP	
EXPECT		FRONT		HER	
EXPERIENCE		FULL		HERE	
EXPERT		FULLY		HIGH	
EXPRESS		FURTHER		HIM	
EYE		FUTURE		HIMSELF	
FACE		GAVE		HIS	
FACT		GENERAL		HISTORY	
FALL		GENTLEMEN		HOLD	
FAMILY		GET		HOLE	
FAR		GIRL		HOME	
FARM		GIVE		HOPE	
FATHER		GO		HORSE	
FEAR		GOLD		HOUR	
FEBRUARY		GOOD		HOUSE	
FEEL		GOVERN		HOW	
FEW		GOVERNMENT		HOWEVER	
FIELD		GREAT		HUNDRED	
FIGURE		GROUND		I	
FINAL		GROW		IDEA	
FIND		HAD		IF	
FIRE		HALF		IMMEDIATE	
FIRST		HAND		IMPORTANT	
FISH		HAPPEN		IMPOSSIBLE	
FLY		HAPPY		IMPROVE	
FOLLOW		HARD		IN	
FOOD		HAS		INCREASE	
FOOT		HAVE		INDEED	
FOR		HE		INDUSTRY	
FORCE		HEAD		INFLUENCE	
FORM		HEALTH		INFORM	
FORWARD		HEAR		INFORMATION	
FREE		HEART		INSTRUCTION	
FREQUENT		HEAT		INSURANCE	

3

INTEREST		LINE		MILK	
IRON		LIST		MILLION	
IS		LITTLE		MIND	
ISSUE		LIVE		MINE	
IT		LONG		MINUTE	
ITSELF		LONGER		MISS	
JANUARY		LOOK		MODERN	
JUDGE		LOSS		MOMENT	
JULY		LOVE		MONDAY	
JUNE		LOW		MONEY	
JUST		MACHINE		MONTH	
KEEP		MADE } MAID }		MORE	
KIND				MORNING	
KING		MAKE		MOST	
KNEW		MAN		MOTHER	
KNOW		MANUFAC- TURE		MOTOR	
KNOWLEDGE		MANY		MOVE	
LABOUR		MARCH		MR.	
LAND		MARK		MUCH	
LANGUAGE		MARKET		MUST	
LARGE		MARRY		MY	
LAST		MASS		MYSELF	
LATE		MASTER		NAME	
LAW		MATTER		NATION	
LEAD		MAY		NATURE	
LEARN		ME		NEAR	
LEAST		MEAL		NECESSARY	
LEAVE		MEAN		NEED	
LEFT		MEASURE		NEITHER	
LESS		MEAT } MEET }		NEVER	
LET				NEW	
LETTER		MEMBER		NEWS	
LIFE		MEMORY		NEXT	
LIGHT		METHOD		NIGHT	
LIKE		MIGHT		NO	
LIMIT		MILE		NOR	

4

NORTH	OUT	PRESENT	
NOT	OVER	PRICE	
NOTE	OWE	PRINCIPLE	
NOTHING	OWN	PROBABLE	
NOVEMBER	PAGE	PRODUCT	
NOW	PAINT	PROFIT	
NUMBER	PAPER	PROPERTY	
OBJECT	PART	PROVIDE	
OBSERVATION	PARTICULAR	PUBLIC	
OCTOBER	PARTY	PUBLISH	
OF	PASS	PULL	
OFF	PAY	PURPOSE	
OFFER	PEACE	PUT	
OFFICE	PENCE	QUALITY	
OFFICIAL	PEOPLE	QUARTER	
OFTEN	PERFECT	QUESTION	
OH!	PERHAPS	QUICK	
OIL	PERSON	QUITE	
OLD	PERSONAL	RADIO	
ON	PICTURE	RAIL	
ONCE	PIECE	RATE	
ONE	PLACE	RATHER	
ONLY	PLAIN	REACH	
OPEN	PLAN	READ	
OPERATE	PLANE	READY	
OPINION	PLANT	REAL	
OPPORTUNITY	PLAY	REALLY	
OR	PLEASE	REASON	
ORDER	PLEASURE	RECEIVE	
ORGANIZE	POINT	RECENT	
ORGANIZA-TION	POLITICAL	RECORD	
OTHER	POOR	RED	
OUGHT	POSITION	REGARD	
OUR	POSSIBLE	REGRET	
OURSELVES	POUND	REGULAR	
	POWER	RELATE	

5

REMARK	SELF	SPEAK
REMEMBER	SELL	SPECIAL
REPORT	SEND	SPEND } SPENT }
REPRESENT	SENSE	STAND
REQUIRE	SENT	START
RESPECT	SEPTEMBER	STATE
RESPONSIBLE } RESPONSI- BILITY }	SERIOUS	STATION
	SERVE	STEAL } STEEL }
REST	SERVICE	STEP
RESULT	SET	STILL
RETURN	SEVERAL	STONE
RIGHT	SEW	STOP
RIVER	SHALL	STORE
ROAD	SHE	STORY
ROOM	SHIP	STRAIGHT
ROUND	SHORT	STRANGE
RULE	SHOULD	STREET
RUN	SHOW	STRONG
SAFE	SIDE	SUBJECT
SAID	SIGN	SUCCESS
SAIL } SALE }	SIMPLE	SUCH
	SINCE	SUGGEST
SAME	SIR	SUM
SATISFAC- TORY	SIT	SUMMER
SATURDAY	SITUATION	SUNDAY
SAVE	SIX	SUPPLY
SAY	SIZE	SUPPORT
SCENE	SMALL	SURE
SCHOOL	SO	SURPRISE
SCIENCE	SOME	SWEET
SEA	SOMETIMES	SYSTEM
SECOND	SOON	TABLE
SEE	SORT	TAKE
SEEM	SOUND	TALK
SEEN	SOUTH	
	SOW	

6

TAX	TOWN	WEIGH	
TEACH	TRADE	WELL	
TELEVISION	TRAIN	WENT	
TELL	TROUBLE	WERE	
TEST	TRUE	WEST	
THAN	TRUST	WHAT	
THANK	TRUTH	WHATEVER	
THAT	TRY	WHEN	
THE	TUESDAY	WHENEVER	
THEIR	TURN	WHERE	
THEM	UNDER	WHETHER	
THEMSELVES	UNTIL	WHICH	
THEN	UP	WHILE	
THERE	UPON	WHITE	
THEREFORE	US	WHO	
THESE	USE	WHOLE	
THEY	USUAL	WHOM	
THING	VALUE	WHOSE	
THINK	VERY	WHY	
THIRD	VIEW	WIDE	
THIS	VOICE	WILL	
THOSE	WAIST	WINDOW	
THOUGH	WALK	WINTER	
THOUGHT	WANT	WIRE	
THOUSAND	WAR	WISE	
THROUGH	WARM	WISH	
THURSDAY	WAS	WITH	
TILL	WASTE	WITHIN	
TIME	WATCH	WITHOUT	
TO	WATER	WOMAN	
TOGETHER	WAY	WOMEN	
TOLD	WE	WONDERFUL / WONDERFULLY	
TOMORROW	WEAK		
TOO	WEATHER	WORD	
TOUCH	WEDNESDAY	WORK	
TOWARD	WEEK	WORLD	

7

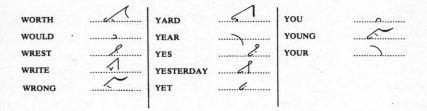

WORTH		YARD	YOU
WOULD		YEAR	YOUNG
WREST		YES	YOUR
WRITE		YESTERDAY	
WRONG		YET	

DERIVATIVE OUTLINES

THESE DERIVATIVES, TOGETHER WITH THE ROOT WORDS,
REPRESENT APPROXIMATELY 80 PER CENT OF THE WORDS
CONTAINED IN ORDINARY ENGLISH MATTER

ably	against	amongst	
accounts	ages	amounts	
accounting	aged	amounting	
acts	ageing	animals	
acting			
action	agrees	announces	
	agreed	announced	
actions	agreeing	announcing	
adds	agreeable	announce-ment	
added	agreeably		
adding	agreement	announce-ments	
addition	agreements		
additions		announcer	
additional	airplane	announcers	
advantages	airplanes	answers	
	airs	answered	
advertised	airy	answering	
advertisement			
advertising	almost	anybody	
	already	anyone	
afterwards	although	anything	
afternoons	always	anywhere	

8

appears	bases	brakes } breaks }
appeared	based	
appearing	basing	braking } breaking }
	basic	broke
arms	basis	broken
armed	beautifully	
arming		brings
army	became	bringing
armies	becomes	
		brothers
arts	beds	
		builds
asks	been	buildings
asked		
asking	begins	buoys
	beginning	
attempts	began	burns
attempting	begun	burned
		burnt
authorities	believed	burning
authoritative	believing	
		businesses
babies	bigger	
babyish	biggest	buys
		buying
backs	blackness	buyer
backed		buyers
backing	boards	
backward	boarding	calls
backwards		called
background	bodies	calling
	bodily	
badly		cannot
	books	
balances	booked	capitals
balanced	booking	capitalist
balancing		capitalists
	boys	
banks	boyhood	cares
banked	boyish	cared
banking		

9

caring	checks } cheques }	comfortable
careful		comfortably
carefully	checked	
carefulness	checking	commits
careless		committed
carelessly	chiefs	committing
carelessness		commitment
	cities	commitments
carries	citizen	committee
carried	citizens	committees
carrying	cleans	
	cleaned	commons
cars	cleaning	
		companies
cases	clears	
	cleared	competitions
causes	clearing	
causing	clearly	completes
	clearer	completing
cells		completion
celled	coals	
	coal-field	conditions
certainly	coal-fields	conditional
certainty	coal-mine	
	coal-mines	connects
changes		connecting
changed	coldly	connection
changing	coldness	connections
changeless		
	colours	considers
characters	colouring	considered
	colourless	considering
charges	colourful	consideration
charged		considerations
charging	comes	considerable
	coming	considerably
cheaper		
cheapest	comforts	continues
cheaply	comforting	continued
cheapness		continuing

10

continuance	dates	developing
continual	dating	development
continually	days	developments
continuous	daily	
controls	daylight	dies
controlling	dearer	died
copies	dearest	dying
copied	dearly	differences
copying	deeper	different
costs	deepest	differed
costing	deeply	differing
countries	degrees	difficulties
countryside	delivered	directs
courses	delivers	directing
covers	deliveries	directly
covered	delivering	director
covering	delivery	directors
coverings	demands	direction
credits	demanding	directions
crediting	depends	discovers
cries	depending	discovered
cried	dependant	discovering
crying	dependent	distances
customs	dependents	distant
customer	dependence	distributes
customers	desires	distributing
cuts	desired	distribution
cutting	desiring	distributions
dangers	details	divisions
dangerous	develops	divisional
	developed	doing
		does

11

done	effects	everywhere
did	effected	examples
	effecting	
doors	effective	exception
		exceptions
doubting	electrical	exceptional
doubtful	electrically	exceptionally
doubtfully		
	employs	exchanged
downs	employed	exchanging
	employing	
dresses	employment	exists
dressing	employee	existed
dressed	employees	existing
dressmaker	employer	existence
dressmakers	employers	
dressmaking		expected
	ends	expecting
drinks	ending	
drinking		experiences
drank	engines	experienced
drunk	engineers	experiencing
	engineering	
drives		experts
driving	Englishman	
drove	Englishmen	expresses
driven		expressed
	equals	expressing
dyes	equalled	expression
dyed	equally	expressions
dyeing	equality	expressly
earlier	evening	eyes
earliest	evenings	
		faces
easy	events	faced
easily	eventful	facing
eastern	everybody	facts
	everyone	falls
educational	everything	falling

12

fallen	fires	furtherance	
fell	fired	furthermore	
families	firing		
	fireplace	generally	
farms	fireplaces	gets	
farming	fireside	getting	
fathers	fishes	got	
	fishing	girls	
fears	flies	girlish	
feared	flying	given	
fearing	flew	giving	
fearful			
fearfully	follows	goes	
fearfulness	followed	going	
fearless	following	gone	
fearlessly	forces	golden	
fearlessness	forced		
feels	forcing	goods	
feeling		goodness	
feelings	forms	good-nature	
	formed	good-night	
feet	forming	governs	
fewer	forwards	governed	
fewest	forwarding	governing	
fields	freely	governments	
figures	frequently	greatly	
figured		greatness	
figuring	friends	grounds	
	friendly		
finally		grows	
	fronts	growing	
finds		grown	
finding	fuller	growth	
found	fullness	grew	

13

hands		helps		hopefully	
handing		helping		hopefulness	
happens		helped		hopeless	
happened		helpful		hopelessly	
happening		helpfully		hopelessness	
happier		helpfulness		horses	
happiest		helpless		hours	
happily		helplessly		hourly	
happiness		helplessness		houses	
hardest		herself		housed	
hardly		higher		housing	
hardness		highest		hundreds	
heads		highly		hundredth	
headed		highland		ideas	
heading		highlands			
headline		highroad		immediately	
headlines		highroads		improvements	
headway		highway			
healthy		highways		improving	
healthiest		histories		income	
hears		historic		incomes	
hearing		historical		inside	
heard		historically		into	
hearts		holds		increases	
heats		holding		increased	
heating		held		increasing	
heavier		holes		increasingly	
heaviest		homes		industries	
heavily		homely		industrial	
heaviness		hopes		industrialist	
heirs		hoped		industrialists	
		hoping		industrious	
		hopeful			

14

influences		knows		lessen	
influenced		knowing		lessening	
influencing		knowingly		lessened	
informed		known		lets	
informing		labours		letting	
instructions		laboured		letters	
insurances		labouring		lifeless	
interests		lands		lifetime	
interested		landing		lives	
interesting		languages		lights	
irons		largest		lighting	
ironed		lasts		lightly	
ironing		lasting		lighter	
issues		lately		likes	
issued		later		liked	
issuing		laws		liking	
its		lawful		likely	
judges		lawless		likeness	
judged		leads		limits	
judging		leading		limiting	
judgment		leader		limitless	
judgments		leaders		lines	
keeps		led		lined	
keeping		learns		lining	
kept		learned		lists	
kinds		learnt		lives	
kindly		learning		lived	
kindness		learner		living	
kindest		learners		longs	
kinder		leaves		longed	
kings		leaving		longing	
kingly				longhand	

15

looks

looked

looking

losses

lost

loves

loved

loving

lovingly

lovely

lower

lowest

lowly

machines

maids

makes

making

maker

makers

mankind

men

manufactured

manufacturing

manufacturer

manufacturers

marks

marked

marking

markets

marketing

marketable

marries

married

marrying

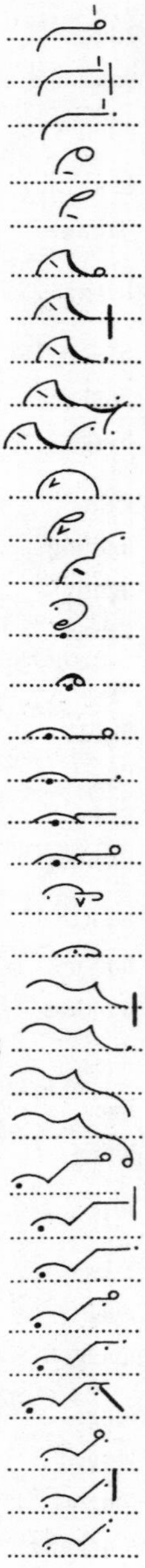

masses

massed

massing

masters

mastering

masterpiece

masterpieces

matters

material

materials

materially

meals

means

meaning

meant

measures

measured

measuring

meats }
meets }

meeting

meetings

met

members

memories

methods

miles

mileage

milkman

milkmen

millions

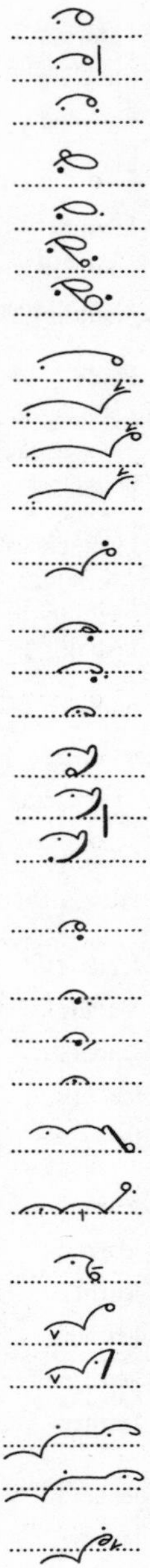

minds

minding

mines

mining

minutes

misses

missed

missing

moments

momentary

momentarily

months

monthly

moreover

mornings

mothers

motherly

motors

motoring

moves

moved

moving

movement

movements

names

namely

named

nameless

nations

national

nationally

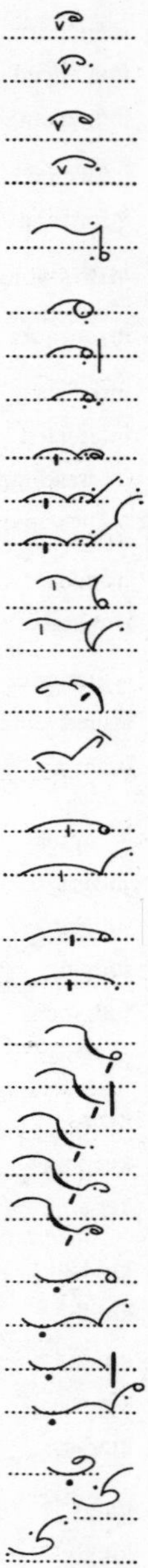

natural	officially	oversee
naturally	officials	overseas
nearer	oils	overtake
nearest	opens	overtook
nearly	opened	overtime
needs	opening	owing
needing	openings	owns
newer	operates	owning
newly	operating	owner
newspaper	operation	owners
newspapers	operations	pages
nights	operator	paints
nightly	operators	painting
no-one	opinions	painter
nowhere	opportunities	painters
north-west	orders	papers
notes	ordering	papered
noting	orderly	papering
numbered	organized	particularly
numbering	organizing	parties
objected	organizations	parting
objecting	others	partly
objection	otherwise	parts
objections	ours	passes
observations	outline	passed
offers	outlines	past
offered	outlook	passing
offering	outlooks	pays
offices	outset	paying
officer	outside	paid
officers	outstanding	payment
	outward	payments
		peaceful
		peacefully

17

pieces		pleasures		provides	
penny		points		provided	
peoples		pointing		providing	
perfectly		politically		published	
perfects		poorer		pulls	
perfecting		poorest		pulling	
perfection		poorly			
personally		positions		purposes	
personality		possibly		purposely	
persons				puts	
		pounds		putting	
pictures		pounding			
				qualities	
places		powers			
placed		powerful		quarters	
placing		powerfully		quartered	
		powerless		quarterly	
plains }					
planes }		presents		questions	
plans		presenting		questioned	
planned		presently		questioning	
planning					
		prices		quickly	
plants		priced		quicker	
planting		pricing		quickest	
				quicken	
plays		principles		quickens	
playing				quickening	
played		probability			
player					
players		products		radios	
playground		profits		railway	
playgrounds		profited		railways	
		profiting			
pleases		profitable		rates	
pleased		profitably		rated	
pleasing				rating	
pleasingly		properties		rateable	

18

reaches	relates	returns
reached	relating	returned
reaching	relation	returning
reads	relations	
reading	remarked	rights
reader	remarkable	rightly
readers	remarkably	rivers
read		
	remembered	roads
readily	remembering	roadman
ready-made		roadmen
	reports	
reasoned	reporting	rooms
reasons		
reasonable	represented	rounds
reasonably	representing	rounding
reasoning	representation	roundly
	representative	
receives	representatives	rules
received		ruled
receiving	requires	ruling
	required	
recently	requiring	runs
	requirement	running
records	requirements	ran
recording		
	respected	safely
regards	respecting	safest
regarding	respectful	safety
regardless	respectfully	
		sails
regrets	rests	sailing
regretted	resting	sailed
regretting	restfulness	sailor
regrettable	restlessness	sailors
regrettably		sales
	results	
regularly	resulting	satisfactorily

19

saves	sensed	sides
saved	senses	siding
saving	senseless	signs
saying	sensing	signed
says	seriously	signing
scenes	seriousness	simpler
schools	serves	simplest
schooling	served	simply
schooled	serving	simplicity
school-book	services	sirs
school-books	sets	sits
school-days	setting	sitting
sciences	sews	sat
seas	shillings	situations
seconds	ships	sixty
seconding	shipped	sized
secondly	shipping	sizes
secondary	shipment	sizing
sees	shipments	smaller
seeing	shipbuilding	smallest
saw	shipyard	somehow
seems	shipyards	something
seemed	shortest	somewhere
seemly	shortly	sorts
sells	shorthand	sorting
selling	shows	sounds
seller	showed	sounding
sellers	showing	south-west
selves	shown	sows
sends	showroom	
sending	showrooms	

20

speaks	stories	systems
speaking	straightfor-ward	tables
specially		takes
spends	strangest	taking
spending	strangely	taken
stands	streets	took
standing	strongly	talks
starts		talking
starting	subjected	talked
stated	successes	taxes
stating	successful	taxed
states	successfully	taxing
statesman	suggests	taxation
statesmen	suggesting	teaches
statement	suggestion	teaching
statements	sums	teacher
stations	summed	teachers
stealing } steeling }	summing	tells
steals } steels }	summers	telling
steps	supplies	tests
stepped	supplied	testing
stepping	supplying	thanked
stones	supports	thanking
stony	supporting	thankful
stops	surely	thankfulness
stopped	surprises	thankless
stopping	surprised	thanklessness
stores	surprising	things
stored	sweetly	thinks
storing	sweetest	thinking
		thirds

21

thoughts	tries	views
thoughtful	tried	viewed
thoughtfully	trying	viewing
thoughtful- ness	turns	voices
thoughtless- ness	turned	voiced
	turning	voicing
thousands	underground	waists
thousandth	understand	
	understands	wait
throughout	understand- ing	waits
		waiting
times	undertake	walks
today	undertaken	walking
	undertakes	walked
touches	undertaking	
touched	undertakings	walker
touching	undertook	walkers
towards	upward	wants
	upwards	wanting
towns	upper	wars
trades	uses	warlike
trading	used	warmest
tradesman	using	warmly
tradesmen	useful	warmth
trains	usefully	
training	usefulness	wastes
trained	useless	wasting
troubles	uselessly	watches
troubled	uselessness	watched
troubling	usually	watching
troublesome	values	watchful
truly	valued	watchfulness
	valuing	
trusts	valuable	waters
trusting	valueless	watered

22

watering		widest	workers
watery		wider	workman
		widely	workmen
ways		widen	
wayside		widened	worlds
		widens	
weakly		widening	worthless
weakness			worthlessness
		willing	
week-end		willingly	wrests
week-ends		willingness	wresting
weeks			
weekly		windows	writer
		winters	writers
weighed		wintering	writing
weighing			written
weighs		wires	
weight		wiring	wrongs
weights		wired	wronged
		wireless	wronging
well-being			wrongly
well-known		wisely	wrong-doing
wells			
		wishes	
whereas		wished	wrote
wherein		wishing	
whereupon			yards
		words	
whilst			
		works	years
whiteness		worked	yearly
		working	
wholesale		worker	yourself
wholly			yourselves

PHRASES

The phrases used in the shorthand pages of this book have been formed in accordance with the following rules—

A. Phrases may be formed by the joining together of two or more of the outlines appearing in the list of the 700 most frequently used shorthand outlines, or derivatives of these outlines, as: ⌐ *it is*, ⌐ *it is not*, ⌐ *if you*, ⌐ *if you can*, ⟋ *to our*, ⟍ *to turn*, ⟍ *to give*, ⟍ *to thank*, ⟍ *to thank you*.

B. Special phrases are used to represent very common word groups, and sixteen points for the formation of such phrases are listed below—

1. *THE:*	represented by a small tick, written either upwards or downwards at a sharp angle: ⟍ *in the*, ⟋ *with the*, ⟍ *for the*, ⟋ *and the*, ⌐ *on the*, ⌐ *but the*, ⟍ *pay the*, ⟍ *to the*, ⌐ *take the*.
2. *I:*	represented by writing the first part of the sign only: ⟍ *I can*, ⟍ *I am*, ⟍ *I will*, ⟍ *I want*, ⟍ *I went*, ⟍ *I agree*, ⟍ *I trust*.
3. *HE:*	represented medially or finally by a short downstroke: ⟍ *that he may*, ⟍ *for he*, ⟍ *if he*, ⟍ *would he*.
4. *WOULD:*	represented by half-length *w*: ⟍ *I would*, ⟍ *they would*, ⟍ *he would*.
5. *ALL:*	represented by initial hook *l*: ⟍ *by all*, ⟍ *at all*.
6. *US:*	represented by circle *s*: ⟍ *to us*, ⟍ *for us*, ⟍ *tell us*, ⟍ *let us*, ⟍ *from us*.
7. *S-S:*	represented by large circle: ⟍ *this is*, ⟍ *as is*, ⟍ *is as*, ⟍ *as soon as*.

8. *TIME:*   represented by halving the preceding stroke: ...*some time.*

9. *OUR:*   represented by initial hook *r:* .... *in our.*

10. *BEEN, THAN, OWN:*   represented by final hook *n:* ...... *have been,* .... *had been,* ...... *better than,* .... *more than,* .... *rather than,* .... *our own,* ...... *their own,* ...... *your own.*

11. *HAVE, OF:*   represented by final hook *f/v:* ......*which have,* ...... *who have,* ......*you have,* ......*out of,* ...... *number of,* ......*rate of,* ...... *state of.*

12. *NOT:*   represented by halving and by hook *n:* .... *I am not,* .... *I will not,* ...... *I do not,* ...... *I did not,* ...... *had not,* ...... *we will not,* ...... *we do not,* ...... *he did not,* ...... *you will not,* ...... *you are not,* ...... *they are not.*

13. *MUST:*   represented by stroke *m* and circle *s:* ......*must be,* ......*must not be.*

14. *CON:*   represented by writing the outline close to the preceding outline: .... *in connection,* ...... *in control,* ...... *in consideration,* ...... *we consider,* ...... *we continue,* ...... *this committee,* ...... *I will comfort,* ...... *it is common,* .... *in condition.*

15. *THEIR, THERE, OTHER:*   represented by doubling the stroke preceding those words: .... *in their(there),* .... *I know their(there),* ...... *I believe there is,* ...... *some other,* ...... *in other ways.*

25

16. *HUNDRED,*
THOUSAND,
MILLION:
represented by strokes *n, th,* and *m* respectively: ...1... *one hundred,* ...2... *two hundred;* ...1(..... *one thousand,* ...2(.... *two thousand,* ...2... *two hundred thousand;* ...1..... *one million,* ...2.... *two million.*

C. Phrases shown under *B* may be joined, where convenient, to other outlines: ....*I agree,* ....*I agree that the,* ......*I would,* ......*I would be,* ....*by all,* ....*by all accounts,* ....*as soon as,* .... *as soon as we can,* ......*have been,* ......*we have been,* ...*you have,* ......*you have been,* ....*state of,* ......*state of things,* ...*I do not,* ...*I do not think,* ......*must be,* ......*it must be.*

These rules cover most phrases ordinarily required by the shorthand writer in general work.

READING EXERCISES

No. 1

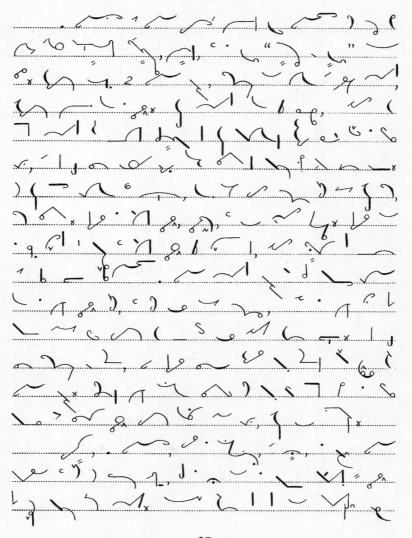

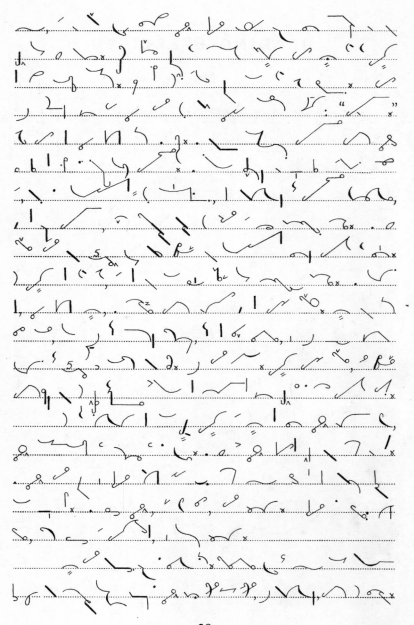

28

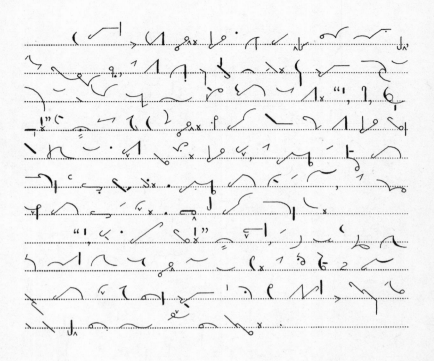

No. 2

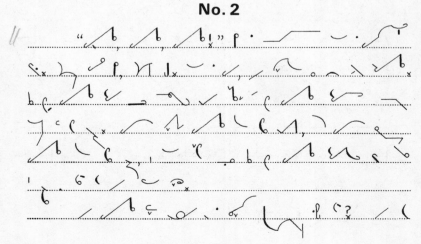

29

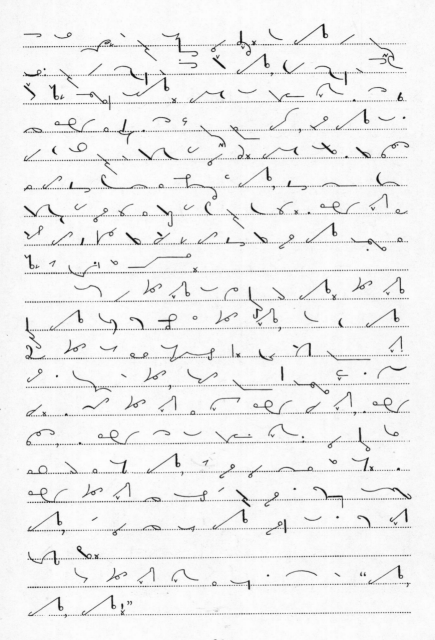

No. 3

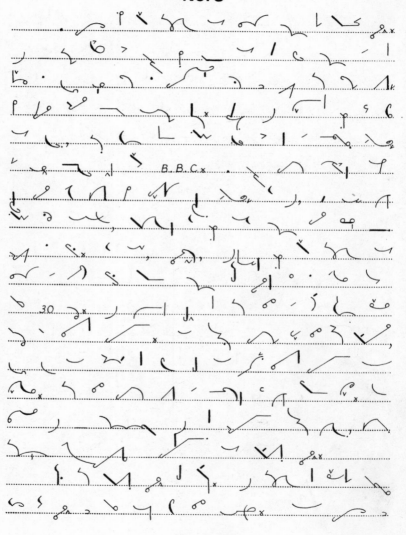

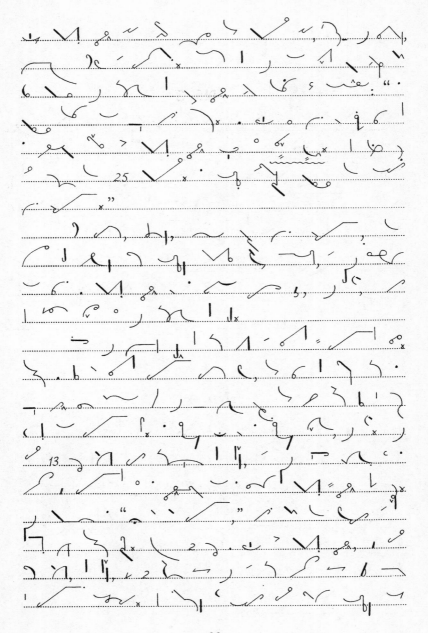

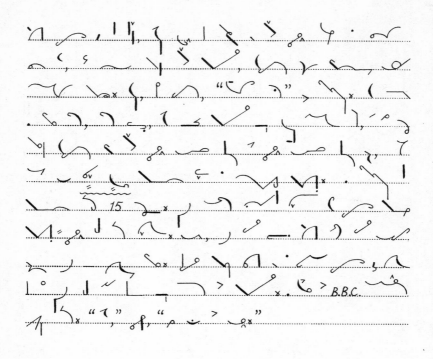

No. 4

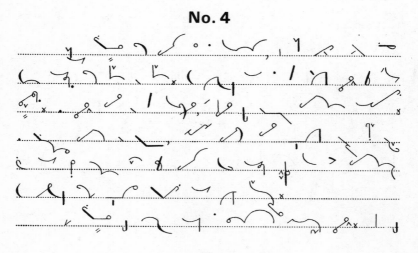

34

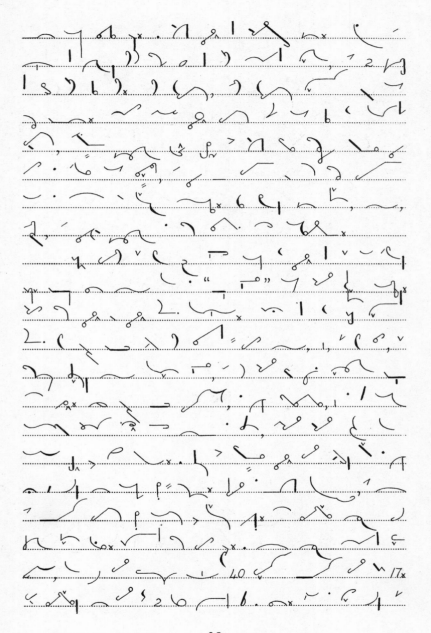

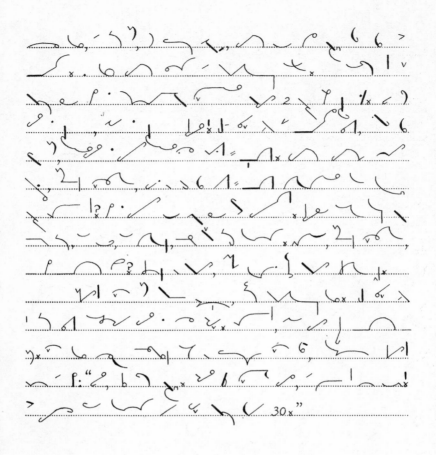

No. 5

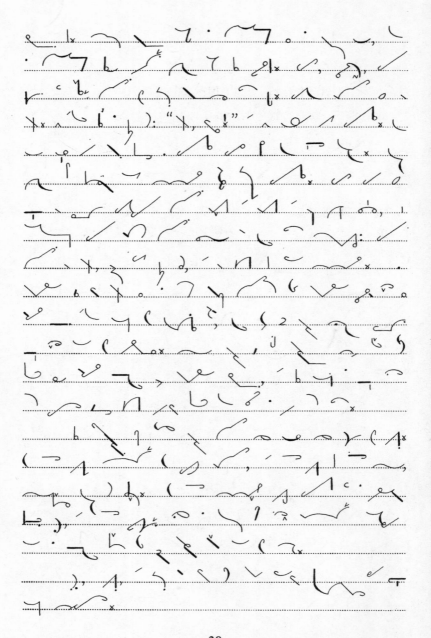

No. 6

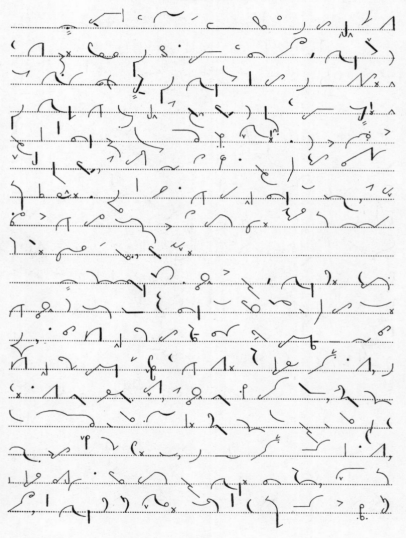

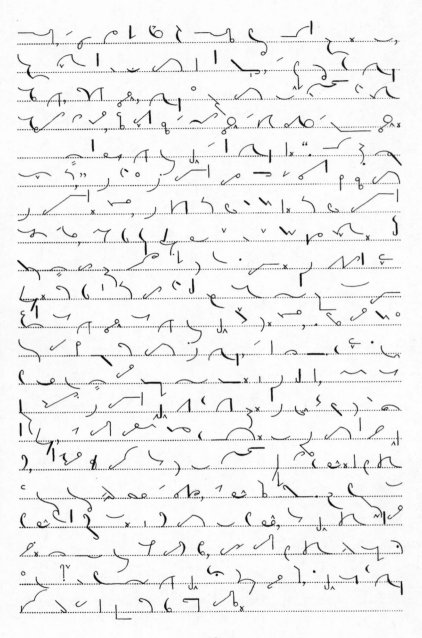

40

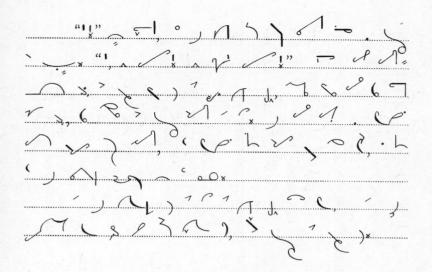

No. 7

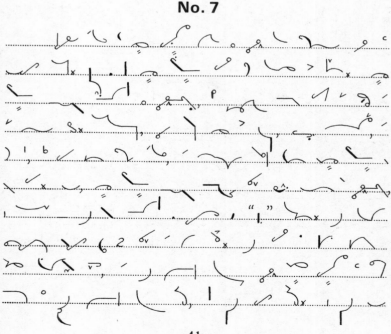

common

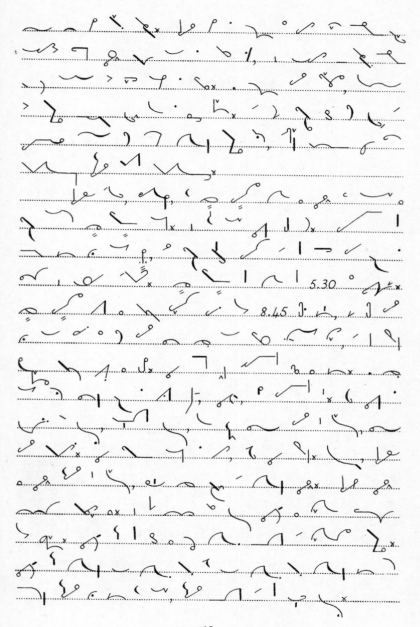

43

No. 8

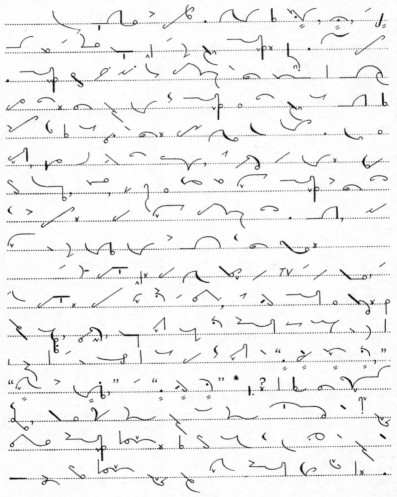

* Richard Jefferies

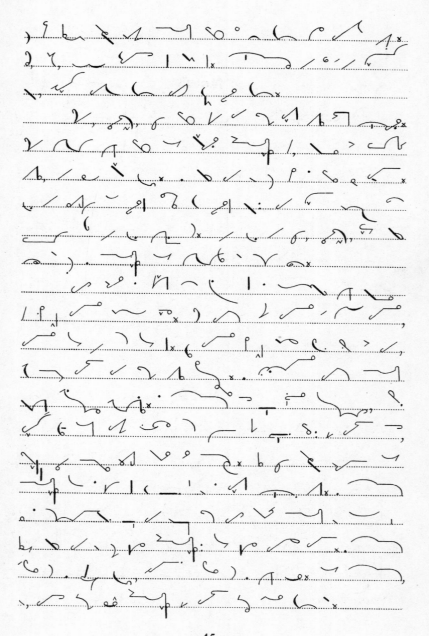

45

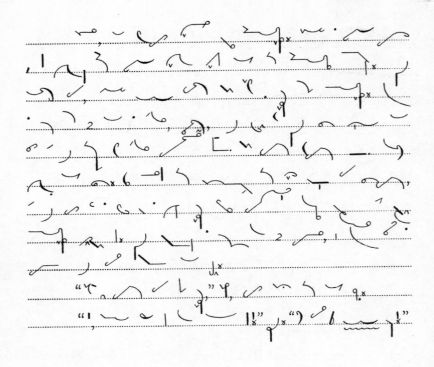

No. 9

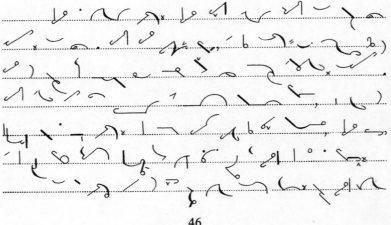

48

No. 10

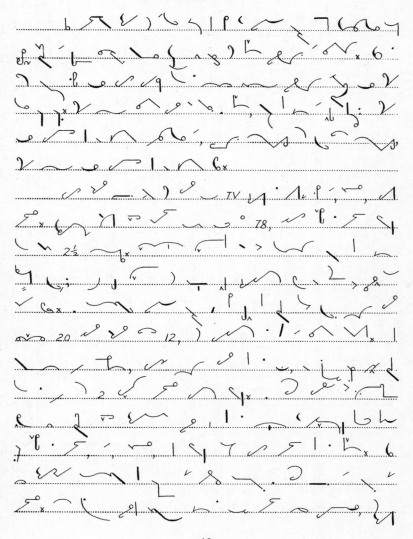

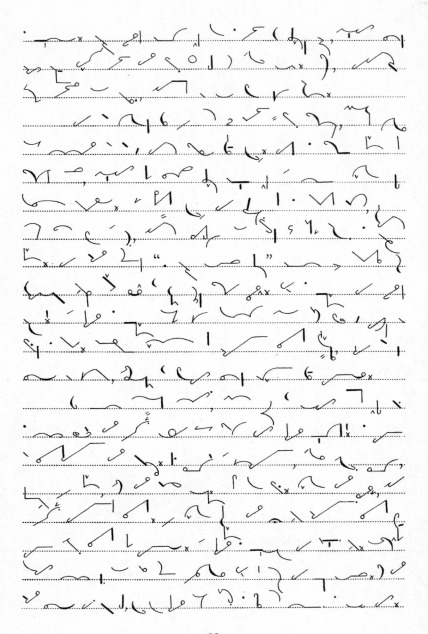

50

No. 11

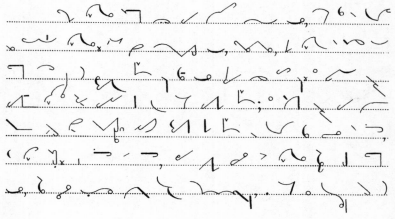

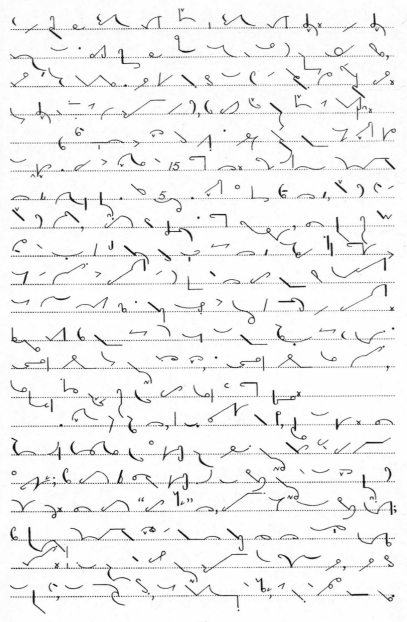

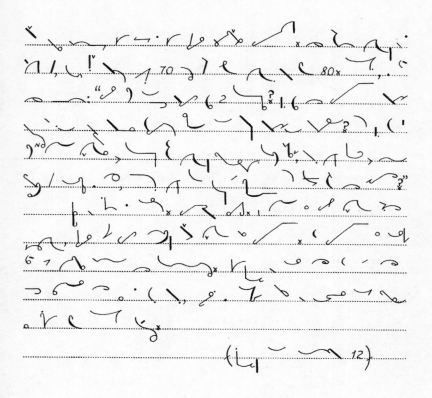

No. 12

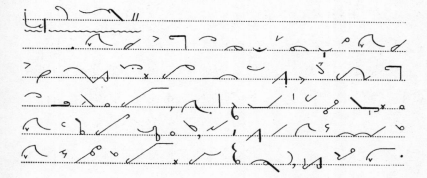

54

No. 13

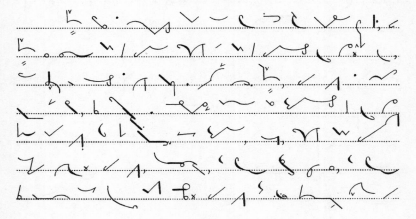

186

No. 14

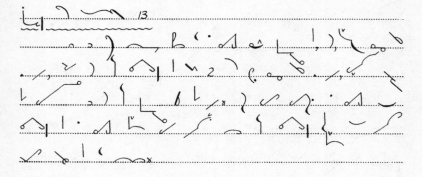

No. 15

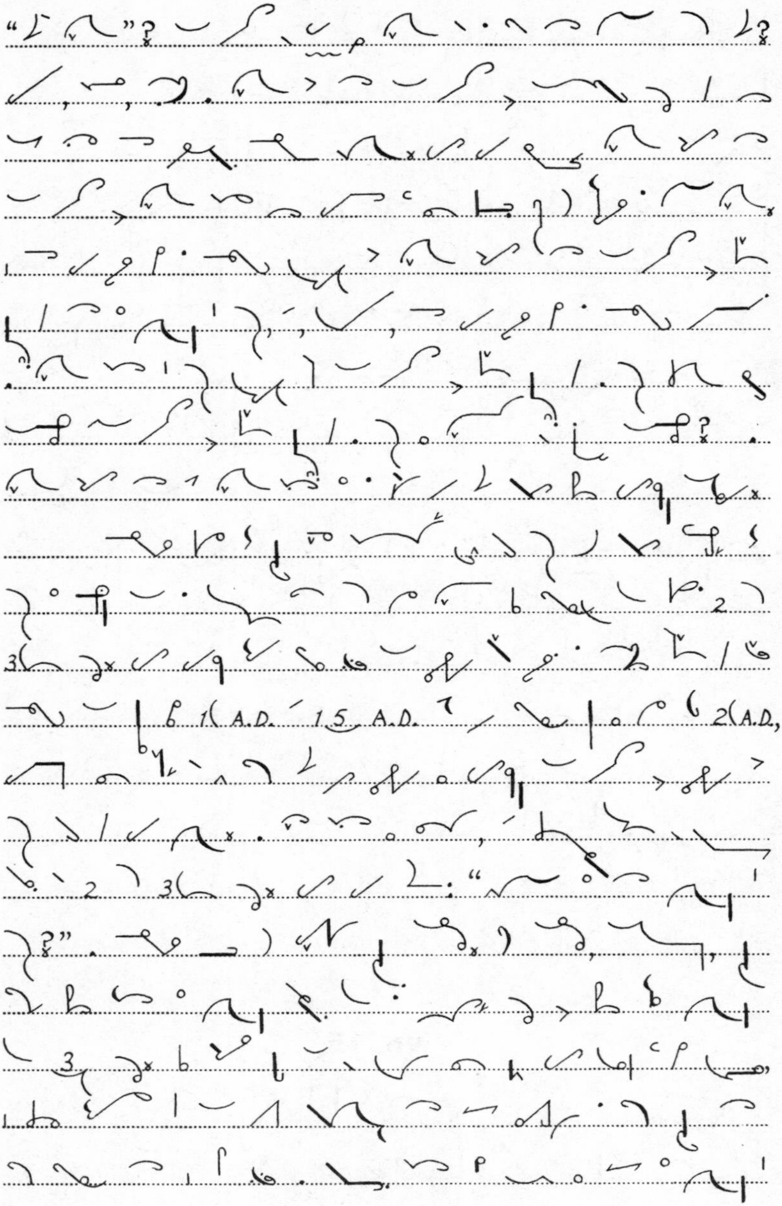

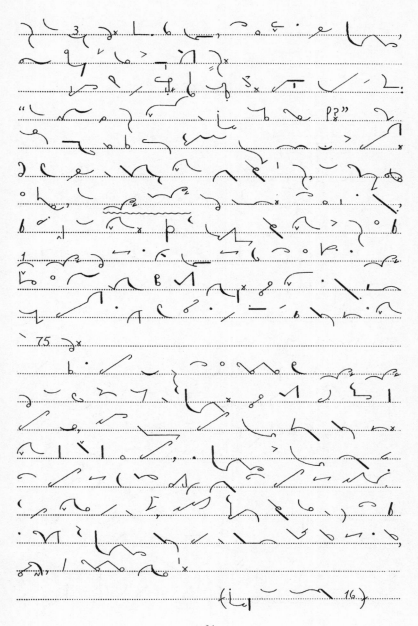

No. 16

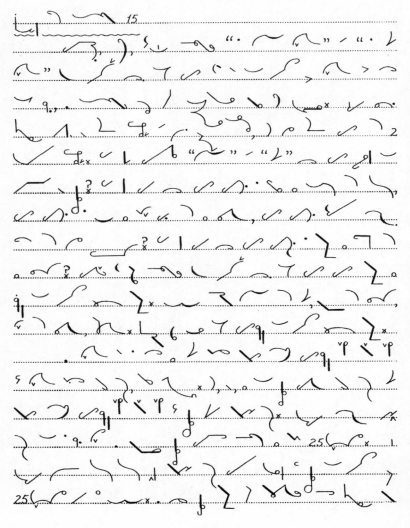

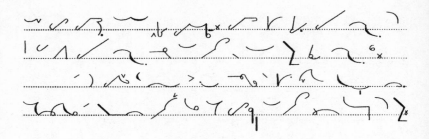

No. 17

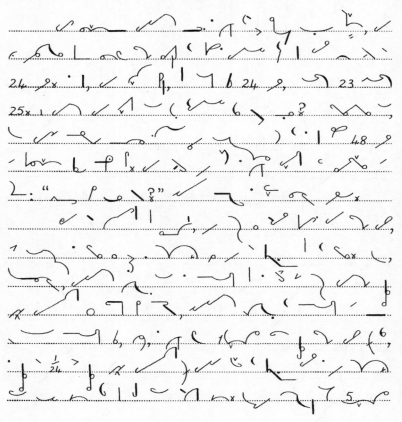

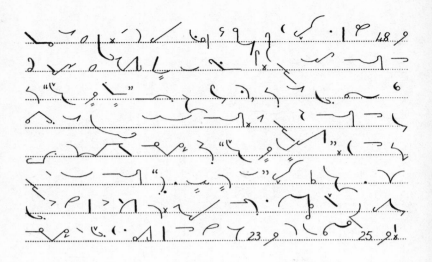

No. 18

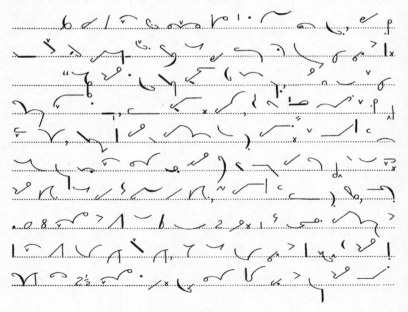

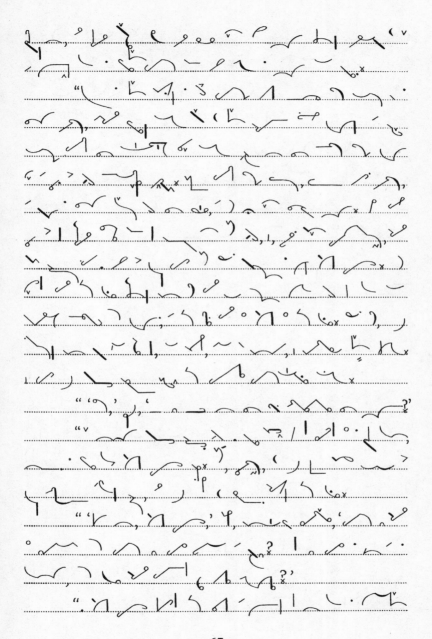

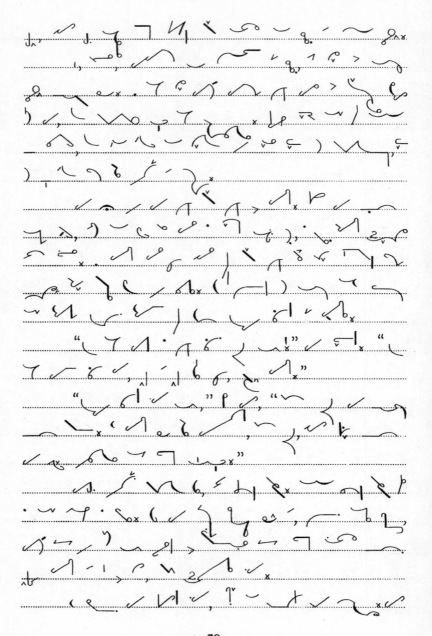

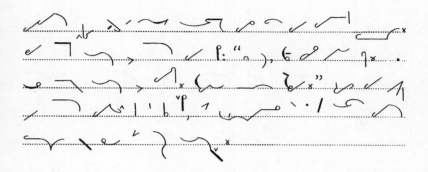

No. 20

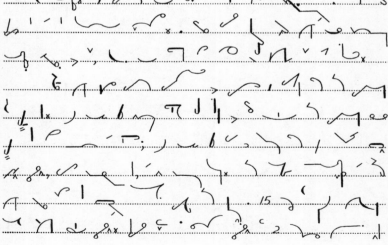

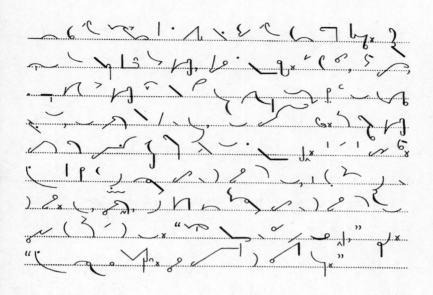

No. 21

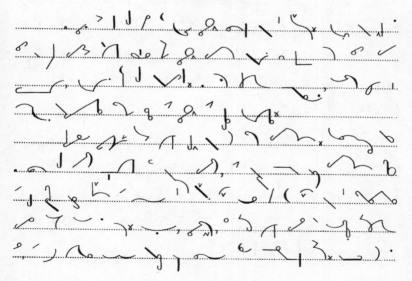

No. 22

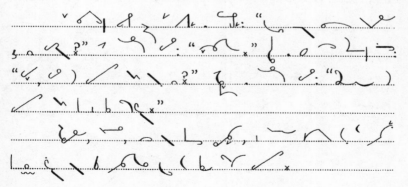

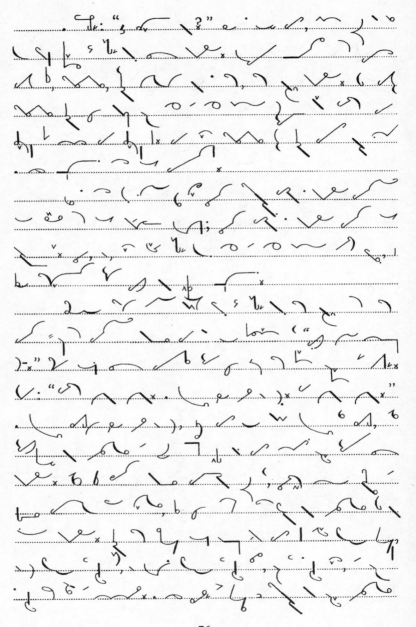

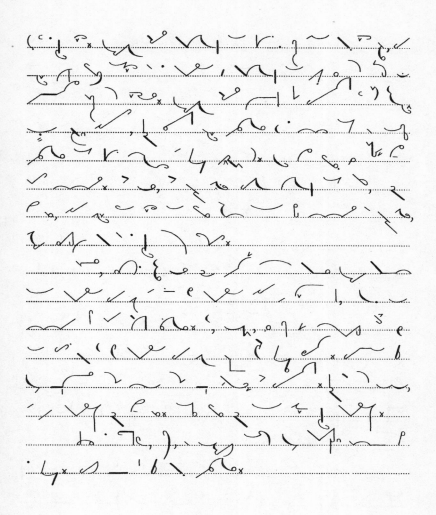

No. 23

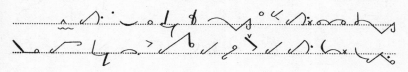

No. 24

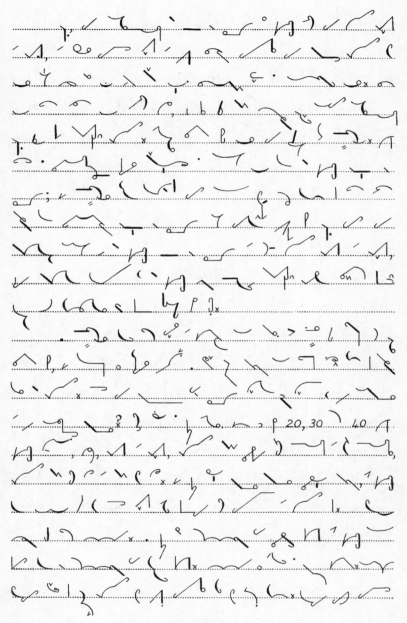

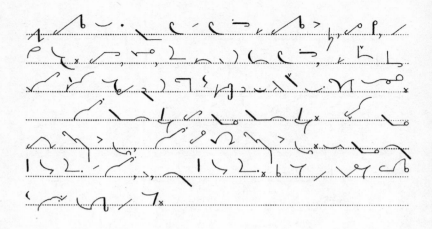

No. 25

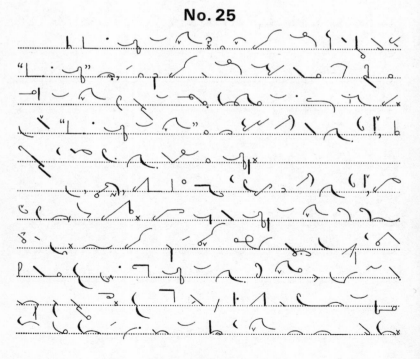

83

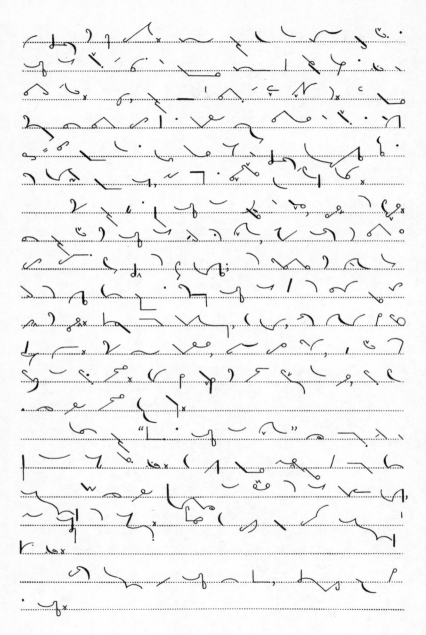

No. 26

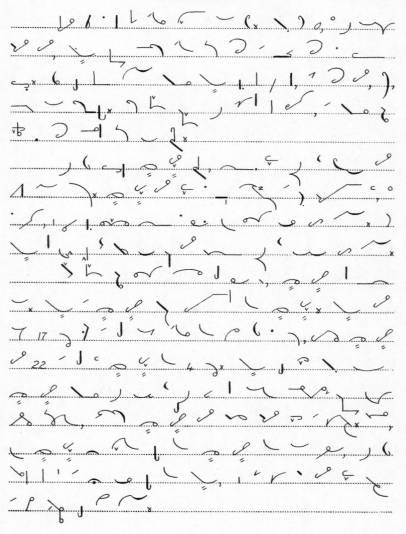

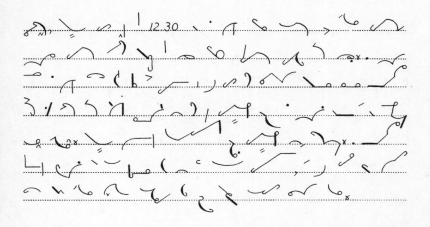

No. 27

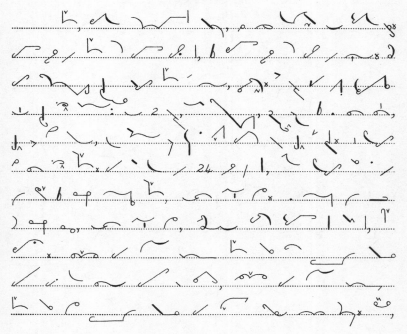

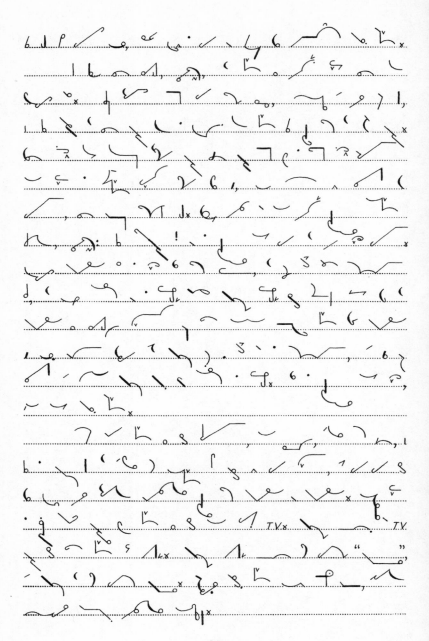

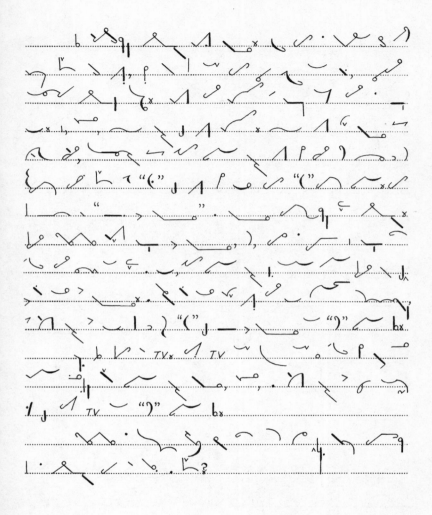

No. 28

No. 29

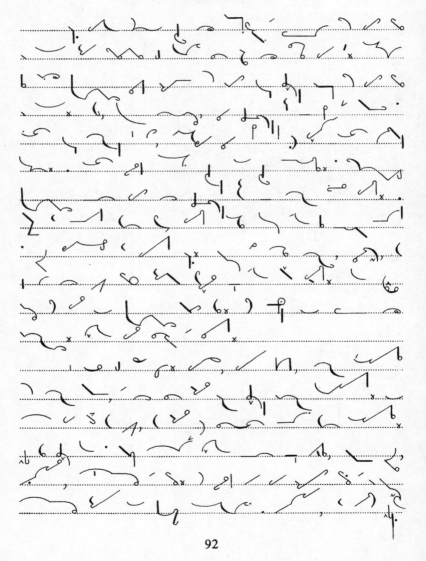

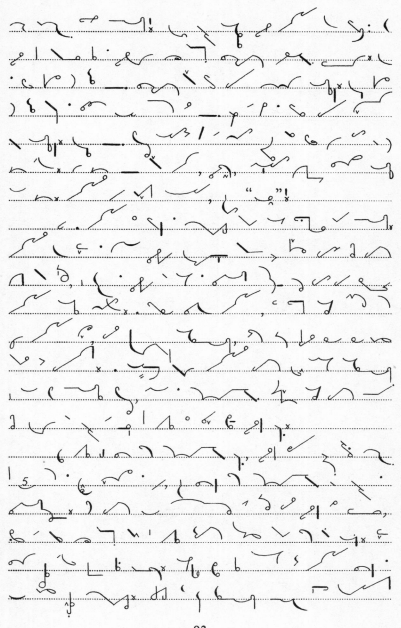

93

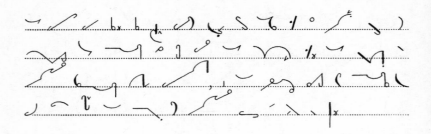

No. 30

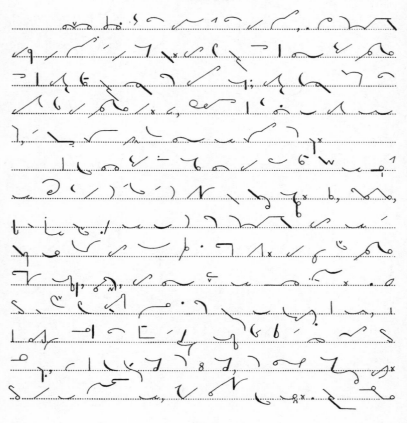

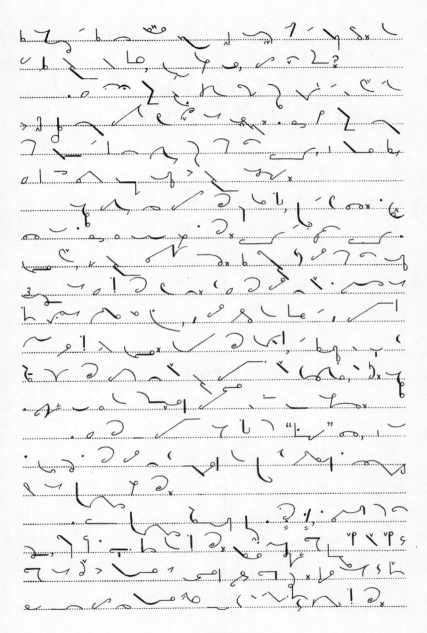

95

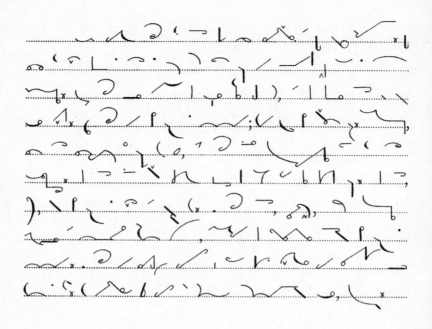

No. 31

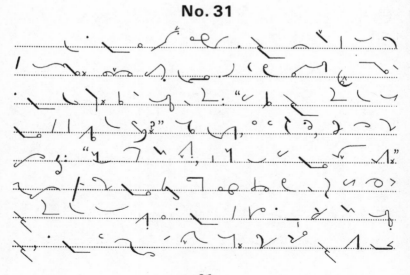

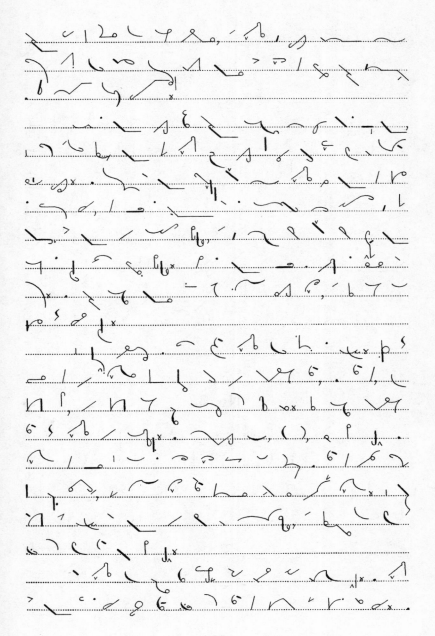

97

No. 32

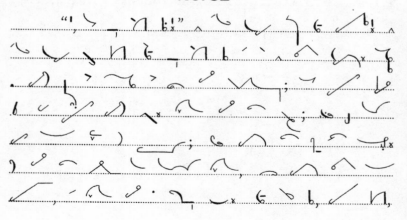

30, 40 50

No. 33

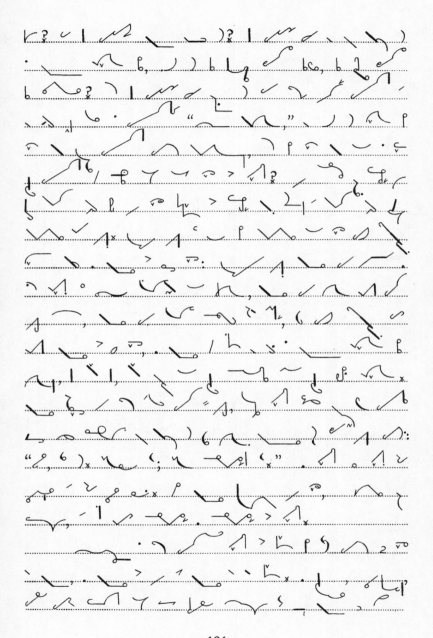

No. 34

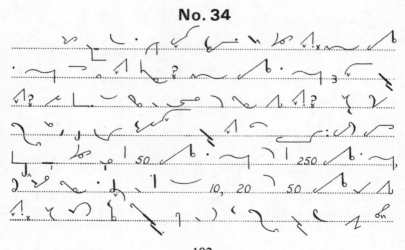

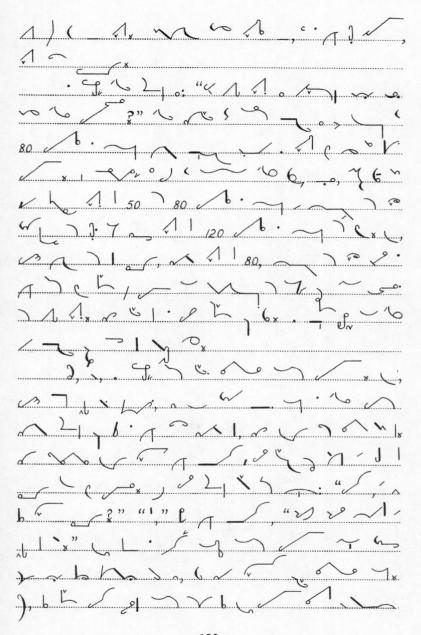

103

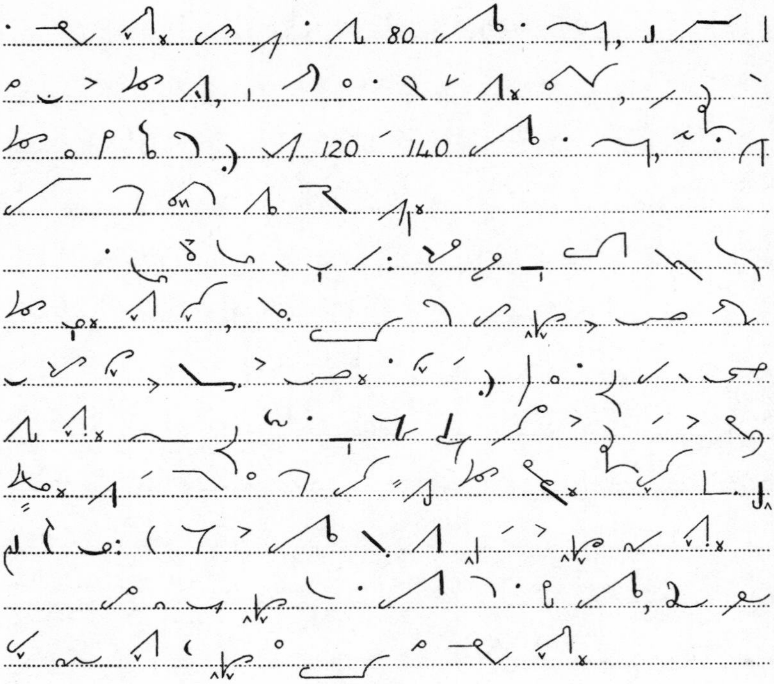

No. 35

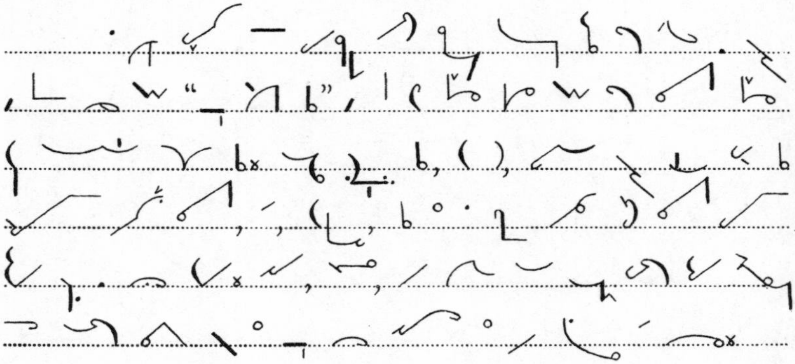

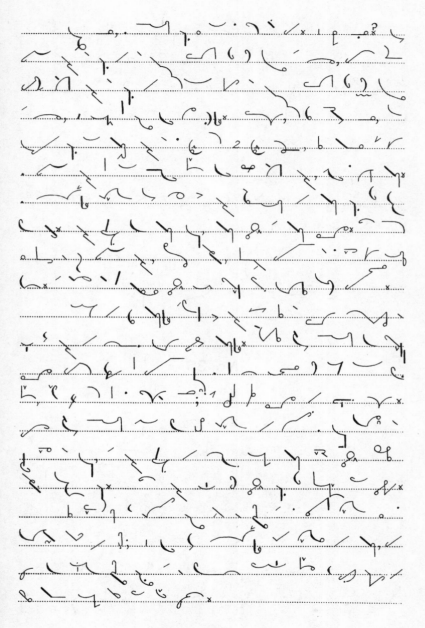

105

No. 36

No. 37

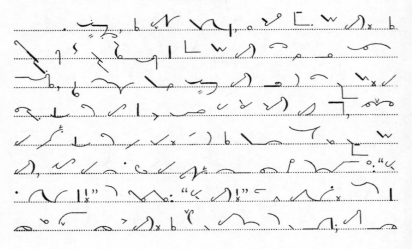

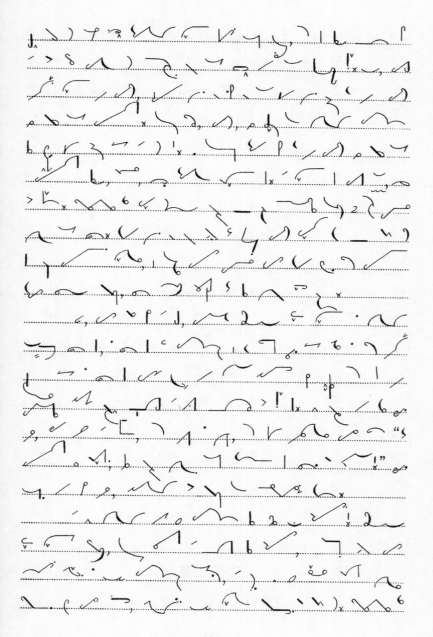

109

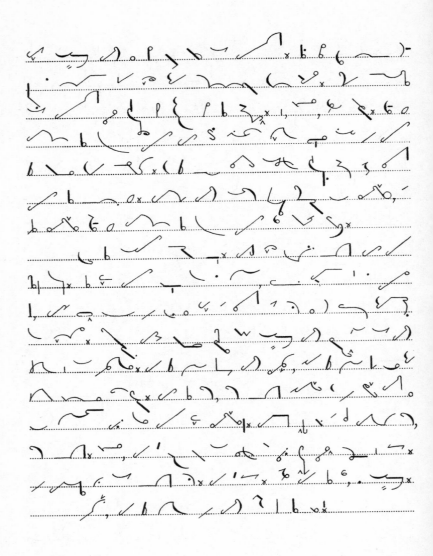

No. 38

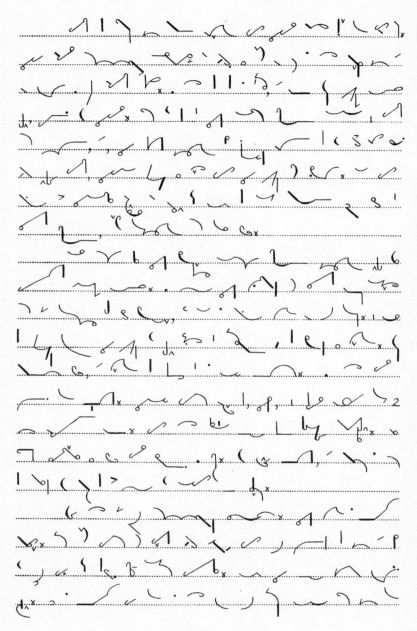

112

No. 39

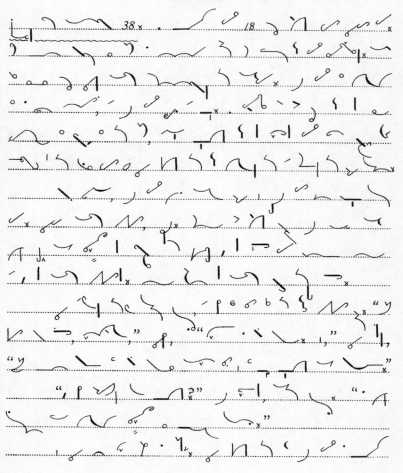

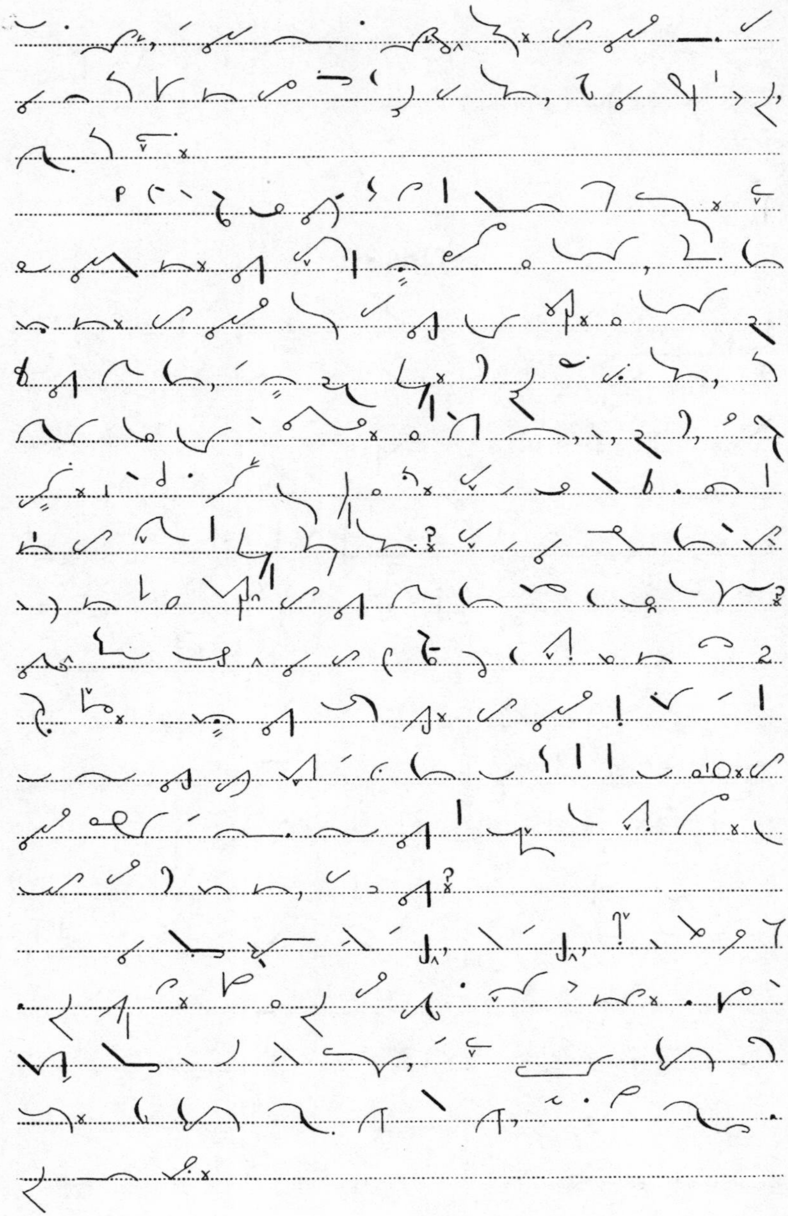

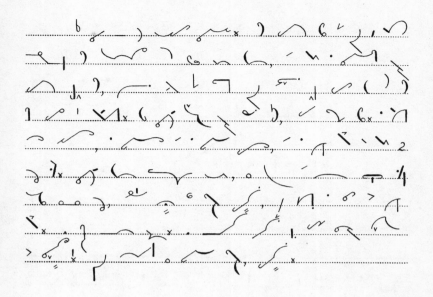

No. 40

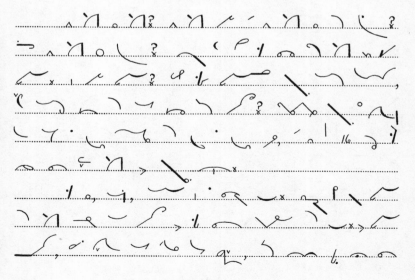

115

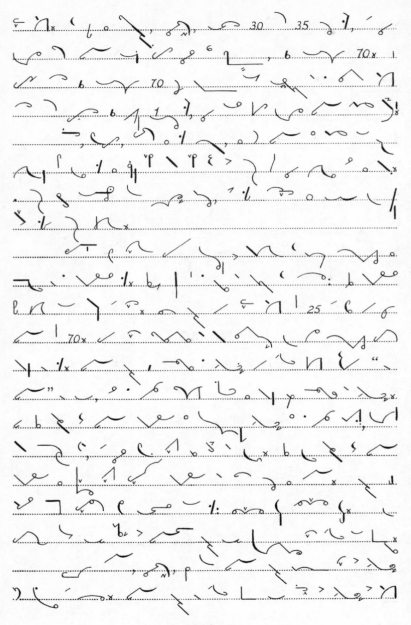

KEY TO READING EXERCISES

No. I

The young man and the young woman looked even younger[10] than their years as they left the offices of Country[20] Properties, Limited, with a few "Orders to View" in their [30] hands. They were indeed two young people, very much in[40] love and recently married, and they were looking for a[50] house. They had been married for just six months, and [60] when they got married on that cold December day they[70] had believed that they would soon find a place to[80] let, and it did not seem necessary to wait for[90] that happy day before setting up home together. So they[100] had gone to live with his mother, having only one[110] room of their own—and they had been very, very[120] happy. It was an old house, however, with no modern[130] changes. It was in a street lined on both sides[140] with old houses just like it, and when April had[150] come and the days grew longer the young married people[160] all at once began to long for a little house[170] of their own, with their own things in the rooms,[180] and with a little land at the back and in[190] the front where they could plant things and watch them[200] grow. It did not seem very much to ask, yet[210] it was something that was being asked by thousands of[220] other young people. There seemed little enough hope of their[230] being able to get such a place because all the[240] small houses were for sale and not to let, and[250] they had no capital.

Will, the young man, was an[260] engineer, and May, a beautiful young person with eyes so[270] clear and true, had been a maid in a big[280] boarding-house at the seaside before her marriage. Neither of[290] them had had any opportunity to save money, and to[300] buy even the smallest house it was necessary to have[310] some capital to put down for the first payment. There[320] had been times during that month of April when May[330] thought that Will had lost interest in her. He sat[340] so often deep in thought and without speaking. When she[350] asked him what he was thinking about he would answer[360] shortly: "Work." And then one day he told her the[370] truth. The big engineering works where he spent his days[380] had set a competition for their workers. The company desired[390] to cut its operating costs and, being a forward-thinking[400] undertaking, it believed that the workers themselves, who had to[410] do the work, might probably be able to think of[420] ways and means of improving methods. The first prize was[430] to be £500 if the best suggestion put[440] forward seemed worth that sum. So Will had thought and[450] thought, and had put in his own ideas for the[460] improvement of methods. The following day, he told May, the[470] employees were to learn who had won the prizes. May[480] put her hands in his, for she saw that he[490] cared very much, that he had high hopes, but she[500] could not help feeling that the £500 would[510] never be theirs. She was wrong. Will won the prize,[520] and his suggestions were considered to be so outstanding that[530] the directors of the company had marked him down as[540] a man worth watching.

So on that lovely day in[550] June Will and May had some houses to look over,[560] houses in the country with rooms with a view. The[570] first of the houses turned out to be much too[580] large. The house was cheap but it was old and[590] would need much money spent on it before it would[600] be any good at all. The second house, on the[610] other hand, was too small. It was a pleasing little[620] place, very clean and well-planned, but far too small.[630]

May was beginning to have a heavy heart. Perhaps even[640] with the money in the bank it would still be[650] impossible for them to get a house to meet their[660] requirements—and their requirements, she believed, were so simple.

They[670] walked to the third house. It was a little way[680] out of the small market town, off the principal street,[690] and the road leading to it had not been made[700] up. They had to walk carefully in order not to[710] fall into the many holes that were in the road.[720] "Oh, dear, this is no good!" thought May—and then[730] they saw the house. Set well back from the road[740] it was placed by itself in a wide piece of[750] land. It was white, and the windows and doors were[760] covered with clean blue paint. The windows were low and[770] long, and the rooms inside were clean and light. The[780] grounds had been well cared for.

"Oh, what a wonderful[790] place!" May cried, and she knew that she must live[800] her married life in that house and in no other.[810] And the hearts of those two young people were light[820] and they seemed to walk on air as they returned[830] to the property office to put down some money and[840] sign some papers. (843)

No. 2

"Words, words, words," said a character in a well-known[10] play. So much was said, so little done. In a[20] way, our life is made up of words. It is[30] through words that we give expression to our ideas and[40] through words that we can keep in touch with other[50] people. We may write the words for others to read[60] or we may speak the words for others to hear,[70] but in either case it is through words that we[80] have been able to pass on to others the thoughts[90] that are in our minds.

Are words quite necessary to[100] a highly developed state of thought? Are they necessary for[110] the development of man to a state of increased knowledge[120] and comfort? Can we, indeed, think without words? Much has[130] been said and written on this last point, and some[140] writers are quick to point out that we can think[150] in pictures without the use of words. Others believe that[160] our thoughts are dependent upon words, that we do not[170] think of the thing itself but of the words representing[180] the thing. Certainly, if we stop at any moment and[190] ask: "What was I thinking of then?" we find that[200] we have been using words in our thoughts.

The use[210] of words is one great difference that sets man apart[220] from other animals. It is true that most living things[230] seem to use sounds of some sort in their life[240] with one another but they do not use language as[250] man does. So far as we can judge from historical[260] records, man continued in a very early state of development[270] until he began to speak. With the use of words[280] he developed more quickly, and when he learned to write[290] down the words his development increased at a very great[300] rate. The written word seems necessary for the wide development[310] of a people. With the written words ideas can be[320] passed on quickly and knowledge, won by experience and hard[330] work, can be passed on to others who can then[340] use the knowledge for their own purposes. At first, the[350] written word could be used only by a few as[360] it was carefully and beautifully written by hand, and one[370] copy only existed of each piece of writing. Now, however,[380] thousands of copies of a book can be turned out[390] in a very short time, and the thoughts and ideas[400] of one man can be read by millions. This has[410] its dangers, of course, as well as its advantages for[420] it may happen—and we have seen it happen—that[430] a person with a powerful use of words can influence[440] millions of people in the direction he desires. For words[450] are powerful things: people are moved to action by words,[460] they are moved to action by the ideas expressed in[470] words. We know that in political life the man who[480] is most successful is generally the man with the power[490] to speak well, to use words in a way that[500] influences people to believe what he says. We know that[510] in business the best salesman is the one who can[520] overcome his customers with words, who can make them believe[530] that what he has to sell is better than what[540] other people have to sell. The successful writer is not[550] always the one who tells the best story but the[560] one who can best use words to express his ideas[570] and the feelings of his characters.

Nor are shorthand writers[580] any less dependent upon words. Shorthand writers depend upon words[590] for their very existence as shorthand writers, for without words[600] there is no shorthand in the sense in which we[610] understand it. Even the old picture writing was a form[620] of shorthand, for one picture had to express quite a[630] long story. The modern shorthand writer is like the success-ful[640] story writer, the successful salesman, the successful man in political[650] life: he depends for his success upon his knowledge of[660] words, and the use he makes of his knowledge. The[670] successful shorthand writer must understand and be able to use[680] a very great number of words, and he must know[690] the words used in a very wide field of subjects.[700]

For the shorthand writer life is indeed a matter of[710] "Words, words, words!" (713)

No. 3

The woman sat by herself in the small room at[10] the back of the house. She could hear the voices[20] of the people sitting together in the large front room[30] and at times a few notes from a well-known[40] air would reach her from the radio set which was[50] always kept near the door. Generally she liked to sit[60] with the others in the evening, hearing them talk about[70] the events of the day and expressing opinions on the[80] news given out by the B.B.C. The people[90] were employed in such different ways and they held such[100] widely differing opinions that she, who knew little about the[110] arts in any form, believed that to sit in that[120] room was as good as going to watch a play.[130] That night, however, she continued to sit by herself in[140] the small and rather plain back room that had been[150] used as an office for the past thirty years. She[160] looked down at her hands and saw on them signs[170] of years of hard work. Not for her were the[180] white hands of her boarders, few if any of whom[190] had ever done any really hard work in their lives.[200] Her hands were red and covered with little black lines.[210] For as long as she could remember she had had[220] to work for her living, helping her mother and afterwards[230] working in the boarding house.

That day her boarding house[240] had been bought. She herself had signed the papers that[250] meant that the house would pass into other hands next[260] month. Another woman would own the boarding house and would[270] plan the meals for the boarders and would, or so[280] she hoped, look after their comfort and well-being. Nor[290] had she any right to be upset about this because[300] she herself had put the house up for sale with[310] the announcement: "A business for sale in good running order.[320] The owner is willing to consider the sale at a[330] reasonable price of the boarding house known as *High View*.[340] It faces the sea and has room for 25[350] boarders. An interesting and profitable business for anyone willing to[360] work."

There were, it seemed, many people willing to work,[370] for letters had been received from interested parties all over[380] the country, and she had been successful in selling the[390] boarding house to a young woman who would, she thought,[400] run it on the same lines as she herself had[410] done.

Again she looked down at her red and hard-[420] worked hands. For her the days of hard work were[430] over, for the sale had brought her a good round[440] sum of money on which she could live peacefully for[450] the rest of her days on earth without doing any[460] work at all. A strange end to a strange life,[470] she thought. She was 13 years old when her mother[480] had died, and she had gone to live with a[490] relation who worked as a housekeeper in a small boarding-[500]house at the seaside. She had become a "maid of[510] all work," running about for everyone and getting little for[520] her trouble. After two years the owner of the boarding[530] house, who was very old, had died, but the two[540] of them—she and her relation—just kept on working[550] in the same way. It appeared that no one was[560] particularly interested in the old woman who had died, and[570] they had found it possible to buy the house for[580] such a small sum that, with the money paid by[590] the boarders, they were easily able to make the necessary[600] monthly payments. They had, as it were, "fallen heir" to[610] the property. They kept the place very, very clean, and[620] they gave the boarders good food and enough of it,[630] and as the years passed they were able to buy[640] the house next door and the house next door to[650] that, until in the end *High View* became quite an[660] important building. The property had become her own 15 years[670] ago. She had never married like other women because the[680] boarding house had been her life. Now, she was growing[690] old and there was no one to whom she could[700] leave the place. It was better sold to a young[710] woman who would love it as she had done and[720] would take good care of the boarders. The voice of[730] the B.B.C. announcer reached her. "And that," he[740] said, "is the end of the news." (747)

No. 4

I did not know the Blacks very well as a[10] family, but I had run up against them in the[20] street from time to time. They lived in a large[30] old house just off the High Street. The house was[40] too large for their requirements, and it was difficult to[50] keep warm in winter. The bedrooms were too big, and[60] when the weather was cold people trying to find comfort[70] in the sitting room might just as well have been[80] in the street outside for all the warmth they received[90] from the coals burning in the little fireplace.

But the[100] Blacks did not move into a smaller and newer house.[110] It did not come into their heads to do so.[120] The old house had always been their home. Father and[130] mother had lived there from the first day of their[140] married life, and the two children had spent all their[150] days there. There they were, and there they were likely[160] to be in the years to come. Modern and new[170] houses were short in the days that followed the war,[180] and Black himself found the situation of the old place[190] very satisfactory because he ran an office in the High[200] Street, and he could walk to or from his work[210] in a matter of five minutes. This saved him time,[220] money, and trouble, and he thought himself a very happy[230] man in this respect.

I doubt whether I ever would[240] have gone into that house had I not offered to[250] try to get some money for a "good cause" in[260] which I was at that time interested. I went from[270] house to house asking for money. I may add that[280] I did not like asking other people to give up[290] their hard-won money, but, on the other hand, I[300] very much desired money for my cause, and so I[310] was able to steel myself to go my rounds. Most[320] people gave willingly, a little perhaps, but a large enough[330] number of small amounts can make a large sum, and[340] I was always thankful for anything down to the last[350] penny. The door of the Blacks' house was opened by[360] a little maid who showed me into the sitting-room.[370] It was a cold afternoon, and the mother and the[380] girl were sitting near to the fire reading. My surprise[390] must have shown itself on my face. I looked from[400] one to the other. The mother must have married quite[410] young, for she was clearly under 40 while the girl[420] was about 17. What surprised me was that the two[430] faces looked just the same. Not a line showed on[440] the mother's face, and her eyes, so clear and blue,[450] were no less beautiful than those of the girl. The[460] faces were small and perfect in form. Never had I[470] before seen such a remarkable likeness between two people of[480] such different age. Yet there was a difference, and what[490] a difference it was! Done high up on the girl's[500] head, above those blue eyes, was a wonderful mass of[510] red-gold. Where were the modern painters, I asked myself,[520] waiting to paint this red-gold loveliness for future people[530] to look at? Such a wonderful thing should be seen[540] by all the world. It was not enough for it[550] to be kept here, not known, not loved, except by[560] her own family. How long, I asked myself, could such[570] colour last? It seemed to burn, and I had the[580] feeling that it would burn itself out.

I turned my[590] eyes back to the mother, with her perfect face. Done[600] high up on her head in the same way was[610] a mass of white. I looked, and not one touch[620] of colour could I see. My face must have expressed[630] only too clearly my thoughts, for the mother turned to[640] me and said: "Yes, it is very beautiful. I was[650] just like that once, and look at me now! All[660] the women in our family are white before they are[670] 30."   (671)

No. 5

It seems to me that there are three principal ways[10] in which we can learn to do things or to[20] understand things—looking, reading, or hearing. We can watch things[30] done by other people, and copy their movements and actions.[40] This is the way in which we learn when we[50] are very young. Babies, and all young animals, of course,[60] are very quick to copy the acts of their mothers,[70] and in this way they learn a very great amount[80] in a remarkably short time. We continue throughout our lives[90] to learn in this way, for we are always seeing[100] others do certain things in certain ways and then making[110] some attempt to carry out like acts ourselves. When we[120] grow up, however, we are able to make observations within[130] much wider limits, and we are free to learn great[140] numbers of things simply by watching. Not only can we[150] see the life going on round about us, but we[160] have also brought right into the home the moving picture[170] and the TV set. There is, perhaps, no more[180] interesting and successful method of learning about other countries than[190] to watch moving pictures that have been taken in those[200] places. Most of us find it much easier to remember[210] what we have seen than to remember what we have[220] read in a book or have been told. Even a[230] very good writer, telling us of scenes and doings in[240] far-off lands, cannot bring to our minds so clear[250] a picture of those countries as can a quite short[260] moving picture. That is why many schools use both TV[270] and the moving picture in the course of instruction[280] in subjects as different from one another as history and[290] science. In such subjects mere reading is not enough to[300] give a complete picture of the material under considera- tion.

We[310] can, then, use our eyes when we want to learn,[320] using our powers of seeing and of observation. We must[330] also, however, use our powers of hearing. To most of[340] us this is a difficult way of learning, and we[350] have often to work quite hard to master the art[360] of learning through hearing. An exception is, of course, the[370] subject of languages, for clearly there is no better way[380] to learn a language than to hear other people speaking[390] it. Mere book knowledge of a language is a poor[400] thing, for a language does not really live until it[410] is used. When, however, we are dealing with ideas learning[420] through hearing becomes more difficult. We have to learn first[430] to pay attention. How often does a teacher say: "Pay[440] attention, please!" And how necessary are the words. If no[450] notes are being taken the words once said have gone[460] for ever. If they live at all it must be[470] in the memories of those who have heard the words.[480] When we first go to school we think we are[490] learning to write and to read and to do little[500] sums, but in fact we are also learning something of[510] even more importance: we are learning to pay attention, to[520] hear what the teacher says, and to hold it in[530] our memories. The person who is able to pay attention[540] is a much better learner than the person whose mind[550] is always going off into other fields of thought, even[560] though the two people may have equally good minds in[570] other respects. Many people who attend public meetings find that[580] their attention is not always given to the person speaking,[590] and it is indeed a good man or woman who[600] can hold our complete attention for half an hour or[610] more.

It is probably true that most people learn most[620] things most easily through reading. They can read the material[630] they wish to learn, and can read it again many,[640] many times if they so desire. They can memorize the[650] written word with a reasonable degree of ease, and can[660] usually master a far larger amount of material in this[670] way in a given time than would be possible by[680] any other method.

Seeing, reading, and hearing all play their[690] part in our complete development as we grow into men[700] and women.   (702)

126

No. 6

May walked with long and quick steps as she went[10] down the short road that led to the sea. Ever[20] since she had spent a week with some relations who[30] lived by the sea in the lovely summer month of[40] June she had lived for the day when she could[50] return. How she had loved the little fishing town and[60] the beautiful blue sea during that week in June! How[70] peaceful it had seemed to her after the cares of[80] city life! The sea to the limits of the eye[90] had been deep blue, and the water met the land[100] with such a peaceful touch that one hardly heard its[110] sound. The ships at rest a little way out seemed[120] not to move, and the white sails of the little[130] ones nearer to the land were still. And that was[140] her memory of it all. Stillness and peace, blue and[150] white.

May remembered also the houses of the people who[160] lived there. They were little houses so near together that[170] they seemed in places almost to touch one another. Surely,[180] a hand held out from one of those small upper[190] windows could meet the hand held out from the window[200] on the other side of that little road. Although it[210] was not really a road, she thought. A road should[220] be reasonably wide, and the houses should be set well[230] back, and there should be room for motor-cars to[240] pass along it. There should be room for people to[250] pass each other without moving to one side or the[260] other. No, she could not really call it a road,[270] but it was certainly a place where people lived. Some[280] of them, like her relations, had lived there all their[290] lives. Never had they heard the call of the cities[300] of their own country, and still less had the voice[310] of other countries overseas called to them. No, for them[320] life had to end where it had begun, and throughout[330] the years they lived in those little, very little houses,[340] lived as people were no longer thought to live in[350] this wonderful land of ours, with its wide streets and[360] modern houses and health services and picture-houses.

May had[370] seen the little fishing town and had loved it. "The[380] call of the sea must be in my heart," she[390] thought as she walked once again on the hard city[400] streets where she worked. Of course, she told her friend[410] all about it. Her friend worked in the same office[420] and until then they had generally seen eye-to-eye[430] about the details of life. That had been before May[440] went to her relations at the sea for a week.[450] She had returned quite changed. From then on her one[460] thought had been to save enough money to take

127

another[470] week with them in the little house in the little[480] fishing town by the sea. Of course, the place was[490] about as far away as it could be from where[500] she lived, and it meant going without quite a few[510] other things if May was to get the money together.[520] But she had done it, and now in the depth[530] of winter she walked down the road that led to[540] the sea. She found that the blue sea of summer[550] had changed, and the water was now almost without colour.[560] No ships were at rest out there, and that was[570] just as well for the sea no longer touched the[580] land without sound. It threw itself with fearful force upon[590] the stones and headlands, and the sound of its breaking[600] would have over-powered any other sound had there been[610] any. But there were no other sounds, for the town[620] itself was resting. Men could not fish in such weather[630] as this, when the water threw itself up into the[640] air as if trying to overcome the little town that[650] made so much use of it, a town indeed that[660] lived wholly upon what it took from those great waters.[670]

"Oh!" May cried, as she held her body hard against[680] the forces of Nature. "Oh, how wonderful! How truly wonderful!"[690] Gone was the water-colour painting of the peaceful blue[700] sea and the sweet little town, and in its place[710] was this great oil painting, this masterpiece of the forces[720] of water and land. She was watching the everlasting war[730] between earth and water, that everlasting attempt of one to[740] be the master of the other, an attempt that she[750] hoped would never meet with success.

And she loved the[760] sea and the land and the little town more than[770] ever, and she would willingly have spent the rest of[780] her life there, by the fearful and the peaceful sea. (790)

No. 7

It was not often that Mr. Wells left his house[10] for very many hours with no one in it. During[20] the day Miss Black was there for most of the[30] time. Miss Black could not be called his housekeeper, as[40] he himself kept watch on the stores and on the[50] money spent. In fact, he bought most of the food,[60] cleaning materials, and so on, on his way home from[70] the office, and merely passed them to Miss Black to[80] put away. No, Miss Black could not be given the[90] high-sounding name of housekeeper, but neither could she be[100] called the woman who "did" for him. She fell somewhere[110] between these two high and low points. She was a[120] daily help of the most valuable kind, and she looked[130] after the house of Mr. Wells with as much care[140] as she would have looked after her own, had she[150] had one of her own. But she had no house[160] of her own, and in the evening she went off,[170] and even Mr. Wells did not know where she went[180] or what she did. During the day, therefore, his house[190] was in good hands.

In the evening there was himself[200] and there was his brother. Generally they were both at[210] home, for neither of them was much given to going[220] out. They did not like parties and they did not[230] like the pictures. They did not care to pay high[240] prices to see plays which, in their opinion, were generally[250] not worth the money that had to be spent in[260] getting up to town and paying for a reasonable place.[270] Neither of the men had married, and neither had a[280] regular girl friend. Their evenings were, therefore, generally spent in[290] the house, and it was the house that they both[300] loved more than any other thing in the world. It[310] was certainly a lovely little house, far enough away from[320] the City to be almost in the country. It was[330] peaceful, and there were good views from the windows. From[340] the outside it looked in most ways much like the[350] home of anyone with a reasonably well-paid position in[360] the City. Few people ever stepped inside but those who[370] did were greatly surprised, for certainly the inside of the[380] house was not in any way like the common run[390] of houses. It was full of the most valuable things,[400] all carefully placed and marked. What had been two living[410] rooms had been made into one very large room in[420] the form of the letter L. The room was white[430] and as clean as if it had been in the[440] hands of the painter that very day. Everything in the[450] room was clearly a show-piece, something bought at a[460] sale and for which a high price had had to[470] be paid. The pictures were Old Masters and the books[480] were beautifully covered. The table and all other pieces had[490] been carefully bought one by one, as opportunity and money[500] made such buying possible. It was such a room as[510] one might expect to find in one of the great[520] houses built in a past age, but no one could[530] possibly expect to see anything of the kind in such[540] a place. The room was priceless, for many of the[550] objects could not be found for a second time. And[560] so the brothers spent their evenings and week-ends among[570] their much-loved objects of art, and tried to make[580] still more perfect that which was already perfection.

It was[590] not often, as we have said, that Mr. Wells left[600] his house with neither his brother nor Miss Black in[610] it. But on that night he had done so. Work[620] had kept him late in the City, and his brother[630] had not been well and had gone away to have[640] a small but necessary operation. Miss Black had left at[650] 5.30 as usual. Mr. Wells read his paper while[660] waiting for the 8.45 train home, but the[670] train was late in starting as there was some mist[680] in places along the line, and it stopped several times[690] before reaching his station. He got out and walked towards[700] his home. The mist in the air seemed to have[710] a red touch, he thought, as he walked on. Then[720] he had a feeling of fear, of cold fear, for[730] without doubt something was on fire, something was burning. He[740] broke into a run, and then he stopped. After all,[750] it was not his house that was on fire, his[760] own most beautiful and loved house. It was the house[770] immediately behind his. But at the moment of his fear[780] he saw his life clearly for the first time. He[790] saw that he had spent his years loving cold and[800] lifeless objects. He saw that he loved no living being[810] and that no living being loved him or cared that[820] he was late home that night, that he was cold[830] and had known fear. (834)

No. 8

After the coldness of the winter months the lovely days[10] of April, May, and June call to us and ask[20] us to go out and see the beautiful countryside. During[30] the long winter the countryside has been resting and waiting[40] for the warmth of summer to make it colourful once[50] more. Some people feel that the countryside is more beautiful[60] in the cold days of winter than it is in[70] the heat of summer. When the leaves have fallen the[80] view is wider, details show up more clearly, and the[90] rivers are full. These are plain facts, of course, but[100] the truth is that most of us like the country-side[110] of the summer more than that of the winter. We[120] like the warmth more than the cold, and we like[130] to see the fields full of the colour that summer[140] brings.

And so we go out. We leave behind our[150] TV and our books, and off we go. We[160] are light of heart and happy, and the open country[170] is before us. Is it possible in these days, however,[180] to get right into the heart of the country—not[190] only to see it but to hear it and to[200] understand it in the way that the writer of The[210] Story of My Heart, Life of the Fields, and The[220] Open Air* did? It does not seem very likely that[230] it is possible, because there are so many people in[240] so many motor-cars all trying to find the happiness[250] of the countryside at the same time. It is plain[260] enough that if masses of people all go to the[270] same place at the

* Richard Jefferies.

same time to find the peaceful[280] life of the country they will not find it. The[290] ease with which it is now possible to reach the country[300] places has made them less worth reaching. There is,[310] I think, nothing that we can do about it. Motor-[320]cars are with us and are likely to be, and[330] while we have them we shall without doubt use them.[340]

There are, however, still places which are away from the[350] wide roads and great motorways. There are lovely little places[360] in the byways of the countryside which, because of the[370] quality of the roads, are seen by few. The best[380] way to see such a place is to walk. Feet[390] are certainly not used as much as they used to[400] be: we like to move more quickly than our feet[410] will take us. Our feet are still, however, quite the[420] best means of seeing the country-side in the lovely months[430] of early summer.

When I was a child my father[440] had a number of little books which set out walks[450] of many kinds. There were short walks and long walks,[460] walks for the hour or for the day. These walks[470] set out almost every step of the way, and they[480] kept the walker away from the roads as far as[490] possible. The landmarks were country buildings and farms and fields.[500] A motor-car cannot go across farmland, stopping while those[510] in it watch the animals or look at the growing[520] plants: but the walker can, provided he keeps to certain[530] parts and is careful. It is still possible to walk[540] in the countryside for a whole day without going on[550] to a wide motoring road. The motor-car is a[560] remarkably good way to get from one part of the[570] country to another but it is not the best way[580] to see the details of the countryside: for the details[590] we must walk. The motor-car offers us the general[600] view, and walking offers us the little things. In the[610] motor-car, too, we cannot hear the sounds of the[620] countryside but the walker hears and knows them all.

Of[630] course, not everyone likes the peace of the countryside. I[640] knew a young woman who had lived all her young[650] life right in the heart of the country's capital. She[660] had never been away, and knew nothing whatever about either[670] the seaside or the countryside. After a year or two[680] in an office, however, she found that she had some[690] money in hand and she heard the other office workers[700] talking about where they were going for their leave in[710] the summer. This caused her to make up her mind[720] to go away somewhere, and she went with a friend[730] to a little seaside place well-known for its peacefulness[740] and the beautiful countryside round about it. She had booked[750] a room for two weeks, but after half a week[760] she was back in town.

"I thought you were away[770] at the seaside," I said, when I met her in[780] the street.

"Oh, I could not stand it for another[790] day!" she said. "There was just *nothing* to do!" (799)

No. 9

It was a lovely river. It was wide and full[10] of water in both summer and winter. In summer the[20] water was usually blue, and its never-ending movement towards[30] the sea was so peaceful that it could not be[40] seen except by the most careful observation. In winter the[50] water often ran more quickly and the colour became blacker,[60] but even so it continued to be a good river.[70] It kept well within its high banks, it was clean,[80] and it did not have places that were dangerous for[90] the little sailing ships that used it as a playground.[100]

Not all rivers are so kind to those who live[110] near them. People used to live near or right on[120] the banks of rivers because they required clean water for[130] the many purposes of life. Today water can be brought[140] to people over considerable distances, and it is not necessary[150] to live near a river to exist. In these days[160] people like to live near rivers because they like to[170] look at them or to sail on them. There are[180] very few of us who do not find happiness in[190] sitting and watching a large body of water. Houses that[200] have good views of a river or of the sea[210] or of any other mass of water can usually be[220] sold at a high price. There is always a demand[230] for houses in such pleasing situations.

High Point was such[240] a house. It was one of a small number of[250] large houses built on a piece of land some 200[260] or 300 feet above the river and the[270] little town through which it passed. A young woman sat[280] at a wide window of *High Point*, reading a book.[290] The evening light played on her golden colouring, and she[300] was beautiful. She put down the book and looked out[310] over the well-kept grounds of the house and down[320] to the river.

"How lovely and peaceful it is here,[330] she thought. "There is still enough light for me to[340] have an hour on the river in *Flying Sails* before[350] the day quite dies. We have so few of these[360] lovely days that we may as well make the best[370] of them when we have the opportunity."

Perhaps she did[380] not use just those words but her thoughts were along[390] those lines as she got up and moved away from[400] the window and towards the open door.

132

"Penny!" she cried.[410] "Penny!"

"Yes?" came a distant answer.

"What about an hour's[420] sail on the river before we go to bed? It[430] is such a waste to go early to bed on[440] a night like this!"

As she was speaking she had[450] run up to her friend's bedroom. Usually Penny would have[460] come running out of her room very quickly at the[470] thought of going on the river, for she dearly loved[480] sailing, particularly in the evening or early morning when the[490] lights on the water gave her wonderful ideas for her[500] water-colour paintings. Young as she was, she was quite[510] an expert in this art. She loved to spend a[520] week or two at *High Point*, not only because she[530] liked the company of her golden friend, whom she thought[540] was the most beautiful girl she had ever seen, but[550] also because there were wonderful views from the house on[560] all sides. To the south there were the grounds falling[570] away to the river, from the north were miles and[580] miles of English countryside at its best. To east and[590] west were large houses in beautiful grounds which, with little[600] changes here and there, made good subjects for her pictures.[610] Yes, she liked spending time at *High Point* with the[620] Weeks family. That evening, however, Penny did not come running[630] from her room. She sat at the table looking with[640] no pleasure at all at one of her paintings.

"What[650] is the matter, Penny? Have you got the colours all[660] wrong?"

"Oh no, the painting is good enough. It will[670] do."

This remark greatly surprised her friend because with Penny[680] paintings did not just "do." They had to be good,[690] very good.

"No," she said again, "the painting will do.[700] But I am not coming out."

She looked so different[710] from her usual happy self that her friend went across[720] the room to her. "What is it?" she asked.

Penny[730] put her head down and cried. "It is your brother,"[740] she said. "He is so wonderful, so much like you[750]—and he did not even speak to me or look[760] at me before he went away this morning." And she[770] cried again.   (772)

No. 10

It is regrettable that we so often hear it said[10] that young people get themselves into situations of trouble and[20] difficulty simply because they do not know how to spend[30] their time usefully and happily. This is a very poor[40] state of things when we consider for a moment how[50] many useful and pleasurable things there are for us to[60] do today. There are many happy ways of passing the[70] time, both at home and out of doors: there are[80] things we can do to help ourselves and, equally important[90] or even more important, there are many things we can[100] do to help others.

When I was growing up there[110] was no TV but we had a radio set[120] and, of course, we had records. These were the old[130] kind of record now known as 78, and one[140] side of a record played for about two and a[150] half minutes. My mother liked all of the family to[160] be at home on Sunday evenings; she did not like[170] us to go out but we were free to ask[180] to the house any of our friends. The number of[190] young people who sat down at table for the evening[200] meal was sometimes 20 and was always more than 12,[210] so we were a large and happy party. It became[220] our custom, when the meal was at an end, to[230] continue to sit round the table for an hour or[240] two while records were played. The machine was not of[250] the electric save-you-trouble kind that we now use[260] but had a motor that required attention at the end[270] of each side of a record, and, of course, it[280] played only one record at a time. This meant that[290] one of our number had to take on the responsibility[300] of keeping the machine going and putting on the records.[310] My father used to bring home a new record most[320] weekends, so that we had a good many. People used[330] to call out for a record they desired to hear,[340] and no one seemed to want to talk while the[350] record was playing as is done so often now. Therefore,[360] we were able to hear the records in peace, and[370] we got to know every detail of them.

We all[380] loved this hour or two of record-playing very much,[390] and I know that it lives in the memories of[400] all who were present on those evenings. We had a[410] very good time at very little cost, and no one[420] had the smallest desire to go out and make life[430] difficult for some other person. On the Saturday evenings we[440] generally had a party also, but they were much more[450] free and easy, and were certainly not planned with the[460] idea of having a peaceful time. We always asked "the[470] people next door" to come to the parties so that[480] they would not be upset by the sounds that without[490] doubt issued from our house. What a good time we[500] used to have! And it was a good time in[510] which the whole family and any of their friends who[520] wished to play a part. I expect my mother had[530] to work hard on Fridays, but we all did something[540] to help, and there is no doubt that everyone seemed[550] to like those weekends.

134

Then came Monday morning, and I[560] am sure that no one got out of bed a[570] moment sooner than was really necessary—particularly when it was[580] cold! A week of hard work was before us. Day[590] school and home work, office and evening school, took up[600] our time, and there was almost no time at all[610] for play. Life was serious, and we really worked hard.[620] Our life at that time was made up of working[630] hard throughout the week and playing hard at the weekend.[640] And it was a good enough way of growing up.[650] Never for one moment did any of us ask ourselves[660] what on earth we could do next. There was always[670] something waiting to be done, even if it was only[680] ironing a dress or making a new one.

I grew[690] up with the radio but no TV, the motor-car[700] but few planes. My mother grew up without TV,[710] the radio, the moving picture, or the motor-car.[720] People walked long distances in her days, but those who[730] had enough money could keep horses. People had to make[740] their own pleasures because very few ready-made pleasures existed.[750]

What we can be quite sure of is that in[760] my mother's day young people did not take up wrong-doing[770] as a way of passing the time because they[780] could not think of anything good worth doing. Wrong-doing[790] was at that time thought of in connexion with people[800] living in very poor or bad conditions and without much[810] hope in life. Living conditions are better today, and endless[820] opportunities for a happy and successful life present themselves to[830] young people who are willing to be good and to[840] work hard. I hope that my readers are not numbered[850] among those who can think of nothing worth while to[860] do in their free time.   (865)

No. II

From the lives of great men we learn many things,[10] much that is of value to us in our own[20] lives. Not the least important thing, perhaps, which the life[30] of almost any great man teaches us is that we[40] have time to do those things which we most want[50] to do. As young people we talk lightly of what[60] we would do if only we had the time; as[70] old people we look back upon lost opportunities and wish[80] that we had had the time to follow this course[90] of action, that line of training. But again and again,[100] as we read the stories of the lives of those[110] who have done great things, of those whose names will[120] be for ever remembered, the knowledge is forced upon us[130] that our trouble is not that we have too little[140] time but that we have too little desire. Our desire[150] to move in a certain direction is not strong enough[160] to influence us to take the necessary steps, to use[170] for that purpose the hours which are being spent in[180] other and possibly less profitable ways. If the desire to[190] act and the will to work are there, then we[200] shall find both the time and the opportunity.

These thoughts[210] come to the mind upon reading a recently published book[220] in which the writer tells in outline the story of[230] the lives of 15 great men. From the many remarkable[240] men who have lived during the past 500 years[250] the writer has taken those men who, by their thought[260] and by their labour, were able to discover a great[270] principle, some deep truth about the laws of nature which[280] had not before been known—men who in this way[290] added greatly to the knowledge and learning of the world[300] and so took all men one big step forward in[310] the long march towards a better understanding of the forces[320] which govern our world. It is not possible to read[330] this book—or indeed any book of this nature—without[340] feeling an increased respect for the power of man's mind,[350] an increased respect for his learning, for his continued attempts[360] to find the truth even when faced with great difficulties.[370]

The life of each of these men, it need hardly[380] be said, differs in detail. Some of them showed themselves[390] even as children to have reasoning powers beyond what we[400] regard as usual; others were just simple children showing no[410] special powers of any kind during their early years. Some[420] were "one idea" men, working only in their special field;[430] others developed remarkable minds and became better than most men[440] in most fields of learning. But common to them all[450] was the power to work for very long hours, hours[460] spent in deep thought, in careful planning, in the perfecting[470] of ideas, and the putting of results together piece by[480] piece to make the whole—a whole which was to[490] surprise the world. Most of them lived to an old[500] age, few dying before reaching 70 years of age and[510] several living to be over 80. Naturally, the thought must[520] come: "Was there any connection between these two facts? Did[530] these men work beyond the powers of common people because[540] they were strong in body beyond the common person? Or[550] did they owe their long lives to the fact that[560] they lived principally for their ideas, paying little attention to[570] the many pleasures which interest the masses, caring little for[580] food and drink or for the company of other men[590] and women?"

It is difficult to attempt an answer. We[600] cannot be certain. But long as was the life of[610] the man himself, it was short when measured by the[620] life of his work. That work has influenced the thoughts[630] and the labours of many men for many years. It[640] will continue to influence man's thought and man's action as[650] long as man is a thinking being, using the knowledge[660] of the past to increase in the present his control[670] over natural forces.   (673)

(*Continued in No.* 12)

No. 12

(*Continued from No.* 11)

The life story of the great man must end on[10] the same note as the life story of the least[20] important of men. We must come in our reading to[30] the point where the great man gives up his work,[40] leaving it to others to carry on what he has[50] begun. His life with all its wonderful interest is past,[60] and we who read are left with the memory of[70] his life and with the results of his work. We[80] know that this must be so, but we do not[90] always like a thing better because we know that it[100] is certainly waiting for us, and it is not surprising[110] to find that there are people who can take no[120] pleasure in this form of reading because they know from[130] the outset what the end must be.

It is, however,[140] no more profitable to run away, to turn our face[150] from facts in reading than it is in life itself,[160] and it is better to take the wider view and[170] to read for the pleasure and the profit to be[180] found in the consideration of the whole life, with its[190] many difficulties and its many successes. In this way we[200] can find both comfort and help for ourselves, whose lives[210] may seem without set purpose, to have little value. We[220] discover perhaps that some person whose name has been to[230] us like a great white light, far away, beyond our[240] touch—that that person met in his early days with[250] many of the same difficulties which we are facing now,[260] that he, like us, had no special advantages, no clearly[270] marked course to follow; like us he had to make[280] his own way, step by step, learning as he went.[290] We find, for example, that one man who became world-known[300] began his working life as a teacher, helping his[310] brother in a small country school. Another worked on a[320] farm, and a third made his first special observation while[330] holding a small and not important position on a ship[340] which was making its way to the South Seas.

But[350] these men did not wait for opportunity to come to[360] them;

137

they took immediate advantage of their conditions to make[370] their own opportunity. In the book which we have specially[380] in mind we find that in most cases the man's[390] work was valued during his lifetime. But the world is[400] not always ready to take new ideas warmly to its[410] heart. In every age there are those who feel certain[420] that there is nothing left for man to discover; there[430] are others who see in the new idea a danger[440] to their own special interests. It is not always easy[450] to look at something new with clear eyes, to judge[460] truly the value either of our own work or the[470] work of others. We find ourselves thinking that because a[480] thing has always been done in such and such a[490] way in the past then that must be the best[500] possible way for it to be done, or because a[510] certain thing has not been done before then it should[520] not be done now. We have to keep a careful[530] watch upon ourselves in this respect, and try to keep[540] an open mind. If we try new methods in our[550] own work we shall sometimes be wrong, possibly we shall[560] often be wrong, but sometimes we shall meet with success[570] which makes worth while all our earlier labours.

Probably no[580] more than one or two men out of all the[590] millions living today can hope to do something so[600] important that it will influence world thought and world action[610] throughout the ages to come, but the methods which have[620] served the great men of any age and helped them[630] in their great work have value for us today[640] in our less important work. By marking the course taken[650] by those who have been successful in their special fields[660] we can learn better how to deal with our own[670] situation, our own difficulties, in the field of thought and[680] of action in which we are ourselves most interested. (689)

No. 13

Time plays an important part in every action of every[10] person throughout the day, yet Time is something about which[20] we know very little and about which we understand even[30] less. If, in our desire to understand a little better[40] the real meaning of Time, we read a modern book[50] on the subject, it is probably the experience of many[60] of us that we understand it even less at the[70] end of our reading than at the beginning—that we[80] know, indeed, very little about the world in which we[90] live. We read, for example, that everything that has been[100] still is, that everything which is to come in the[110] future already exists. We read that the events which make[120] up life are like the stations along the railway line.[130]   A train is running along that line towards one of[140] these stations.   It reaches the station, it perhaps waits there[150] for a very little while, and then it passes on,[160] leaving the station behind it.   But the station existed before[170] the train reached it and it continues to exist after[180] the train has left it.   In the same way, it[190] is said, the things which happen in life are there[200] all the time, waiting for us to reach them.   We[210] reach them and experience them and pass on, leaving them[220] behind us.   According to the writers of these modern books,[230] these events existed before we knew of them and will[240] continue to exist when we ourselves are no more.   They[250] will exist, in fact, for as long as anything as[260] we understand it exists.

We read these statements and think[270] carefully about them, and at first it seems that the[280] statements cannot be true, that we cannot seriously be expected[290] to believe them.   Then, perhaps, we remember some of the[300] things we were told as children and which we have[310] always believed to be true.   As children we learned that[320] many of the little points of light which appeared above[330] us at night are really great bodies which are millions[340] of miles away from the earth.   Light, we were told,[350] moves at the rate of about 186,000[360] miles a second, but so far distant are[370] these bodies from us that the light which we see[380] coming from them is the light which left them thousands,[390] and in some cases millions, of years ago.   Because of[400] this fact, we learned, if we could discover some method[410] by which our eyes could see what was happening on[420] one of these distant bodies, we should see not what[430] is happening today but what was happening ages and[440] ages ago.   If people something like ourselves lived on those[450] little points of light and if they could see what[460] was happening on our earth they, looking at us today,[470] would see not what is happening now but what[480] happened thousands or millions of years ago, according to the[490] distance they are away.   But even when we remember these[500] facts it is for most of us difficult to get[510] more than the smallest suggestion of an idea of what[520] is meant when we are told that everything that has[530] been still is and always will be.   It is difficult[540] to believe that there will always be somewhere the picture[550] of you as you sit reading these words.

If we[560] think of sound it helps us to understand this point[570] a little better.   We see a movement very much more[580] quickly than we hear the sound resulting from that movement,[590] for sound comes to us at only 1,100[600] feet a second as against the 186,000[610] miles a second of light.   Let us[620] say that I live half a mile from a

139

big[630] manufacturing plant, so that the sounds which come to me[640] from the plant reach me about two and a half[650] seconds after the sounds were in fact made. Let us[660] say also that you live another half a mile down[670] the road, away from the plant. You would hear the[680] same sounds two and a half seconds after I heard[690] them, that is five seconds after they were made. (699)

(*Continued in No.* 14)

No. 14

(*Continued from No.* 13)

You would therefore make the statement that a certain sound[10] took place at, say, five seconds past the hour, I[20] would say that it happened at about two or three[30] seconds past the hour, while the people at the works[40] would say that it took place just at the hour.[50] So that when we say that a certain thing happened[60] at a certain time we really mean that it happened[70] at that time in relation to our own position at that[80] moment.

The relation of time to distance and the[90] relation of immediate time to time as a whole are[100] subjects in which people grow more and more interested. Two[110] interesting plays have been written round the idea that everything[120] that has happened in the past is still in existence,[130] the point made by the plays being that a person[140] who has a certain special sense highly developed can go[150] back into the past and experience old and past events.[160]

But interesting as these ideas may be, there is another[170] and much more usual point of view from which to[180] consider time. For all the general purposes of everyday life[190] we all understand time quite well. We know that each[200] day is made up of 24 hours, that there[210] are never 23 hours to the day and never[220] 25. We know that the little hands marking the[230] passing of the minutes and hours move on and on[240] at their even rate, and that although they work in[250] our service they work without any regard to our personal[260] and special interests. They will work no more quickly when[270] life is taking us towards some specially pleasing event, and[280] they will not lessen their rate when we are moving[290] towards something less pleasing.

We know that time influences us[300] in the doing of every piece of work, for all[310] work, to have its highest value, has to be "done[320] to time." The Chief who calls the members of the[330] Board together for a certain time must be ready when[340] the Board meets with the facts, figures, or questions which[350] he wishes to put to the members. He depends not[360] only upon his own work in this connection but upon[370] the work of all directly working with him, from the[380] most experienced man in his employ to the most recent[390] of the office-boys. The motor manufacturer must so organize[400] the year's work of all his men that he not[410] only supplies the day to day demand of the public[420] for his .product but also has his new goods quite[430] ready for the market at the expected time. The manufacturer,[440] whatever his product may be, must supply present demand and[450] at the same time organize future work. Goods made for[460] shipment overseas must be ready for shipment by the date[470] on which the ship is leaving the country. The kind[480] of market in which we are interested makes little difference[490]—goods must be put on the market when the market[500] is ready to receive them. But the principal difficulty of[510] all planning comes from the fact that we cannot *see*[520] time. We have perhaps five months in which to do[530] a piece of work; there seems to be no need[540] for an immediate start and the papers in connection with[550] it are put on one side. When the papers again[560] see the light of day we find, possibly, that we[570] need information from another person. But to the second man[580] this piece of work is something just received, and he[590] in his turn "sits on it" for a little while,[600] only to find when he looks seriously at the work[610] that it requires the attention of a third party.

And[620] valuable days pass until we find that the work is[630] either put through to time as a result of much[640] work and running about on the part of everyone interested[650] or it is not put through with resulting loss of[660] money and goodwill. Even when man has done his[670] best Nature sometimes lets us down, and weather conditions hold[680] up trains, planes and ships, and the "perfect" piece of[690] planning works out less perfectly than we had hoped and[700] expected.

(701)

No. 15

We often hear it said of a man that he[10] had had a long life or that his life had[20] been "cut short." What do we really mean when we[30] use the expressions "long life" and "short life?" In relation[40] to *what* is the life of a particular man long[50] or short? We are, of course, measuring the life of[60] the man in relation to the number of years which[70] men in the mass can reasonably expect to live. When[80] we speak of the life of one man in relation[90] to the life of most men we can with some[100] degree of truth say that it was a long life.[110] But can we use such an expression if we think[120] of the life of one man in relation to the[130] time during which man has lived on earth, and, further,[140] can we use such an expression regarding the life of[150] man on earth if we think of it in relation[160] to the time during which the earth itself has been[170] in existence and in relation to the time during which[180] the earth is likely to continue in existence? The life[190] of one man and the life of man as a[200] whole are short beyond statement when considered in this way.[210]

Experts tell us that the different kinds of material found[220] upon earth show beyond question that the earth has existed[230] in a form more or less like its present form[240] for at least two or thee thousand million years. When[250] we consider that we place events in history by using[260] a measurement of time which finds expression in dates such[270] as 1000 A.D. and 1500 A.D.[280] and that our present date is less than[290] 2000 A.D., we get some idea of how very[300] short our own history is when considered in relation to[310] the history of the earth upon which we live. The[320] mind of man is small, and it is impossible for[330] him to picture the passing of two or three thousand[340] million years. When we ask, How long has man lived[350] on earth? the experts give us widely differing answers. Their[360] answers, in fact, differ from the statement that man has[370] lived possibly for a million years to the statement that[380] he has lived for three hundred thousand years. It is[390] always difficult not to feel some doubt when faced with[400] such figures, but it seems that we must at any[410] rate believe that man—certainly a very different man from[420] present man but at all events the beginning of man[430] as he now is—has lived on earth for three[440] hundred thousand years. Taking this figure, man is quite a[450] recent development, something strange on the face of the good[460] old Earth.

But we cannot stop our questioning at this[470] interesting point. We go further and ask, For how long[480] is the earth likely to continue in its present state?[490] From the answer given to us it is clear that[500] we need not fear the immediate end of the world.[510] There is every reason to believe that life will be[520] possible on earth, in very much the same forms as[530] at present, for *millions of millions* of years to come.[540] Man is but a baby, just starting out in life.[550] It is said that if we take the possible life[560] of the earth as just one million million years—a[570] low figure—then man has at least a million times[580] as long to live as he has already lived. He[590] is like a baby who came into the world a[600] little over half an hour ago and who has before[610] him a life of 75 years.

It is a[620] wonderful thing to think that man has perhaps several

142

million[630] million years in front of him in which to develop.[640] He has already shown that he can do wonderful things,[650] and we cannot picture the wonderful future which may be[660] before him. Life day by day is wonderful, the developments[670] of the future may be yet more wonderful—they almost[680] certainly will be more wonderful— and we feel that our[690] own lives are too short, and we wish that it[700] were possible for us to see more than just a[710] very little of that development before we too become part[720] of the past—a past, however, which perhaps lives on. (730)

(*Continued in No.* 16)

No. 16

(*Continued from No.* 15)

We can see, therefore, that the common expressions "a long[10] life" and "a short life" have real meaning only when[20] thought of in relation to the life of the man[30] in the street, the number of years on which insurance[40] companies base their figures. But we seem at present ready[50] to ask questions and willing to hear the answers, so[60] let us ask one or two further questions. What do[70] the words "long" and "short" mean when used in regard[80] to distances? What do we mean when we say a[90] place is near or far, when we say a thing[100] is of light weight or is heavy, when we say[110] that we are moving more or less quickly? What do[120] we mean when we say that an object is great[130] or is small? We find that all these expressions have[140] real meaning only when one object is considered in relation[150] to some other object. Nothing can be long or short,[160] big or small, light or heavy, of itself. It can[170] be these things only when considered in relation to some[180] other object.

The life of a man is short almost[190] beyond measure when considered side by side with the life[200] of man upon earth, past and future. So, too, is[210] any distance we have upon earth short beyond measure when[220] considered side by side with the distances which are beyond[230] the earth. If we move round the earth in a[240] straight line the biggest distance we can cover is about[250] 25 thousand miles. But if we look far far[260] out beyond the earth we are faced with distances in[270] relation to which 25 thousand miles are as nothing.[280] The most distant object of which observations can at present[290] be made is thought to be 140[300] million light-years away from the earth. Light, as we[310] know, moves at 186,000 miles[320] a second which, it is agreed, is a considerable rate.[330] One light-year is the distance which light covers moving[340] throughout the year at a rate of 186,000[350] miles a second. When, therefore, it is[360] stated that something is at a distance from us of[370] 140 million light-years, a distance is[380] represented which it is beyond our powers to picture. Our[390] earth is large if measured by other objects upon the[400] earth, but it is a small thing of no importance[410] whatever when measured by objects outside the earth, when measured[420] by the size of some of the great masses of[430] burning matter which we see as points of light above[440] us at night.

We tell our friends, perhaps, that our[450] weight is this or is that, but here again we[460] meet with difficulties. Our weight is different in different parts[470] of the world, while if we found ourselves on a[480] body smaller than the earth we should be so light[490] that we could move about with an ease impossible here.[500] On the other hand, if we found ourselves on a[510] body much bigger than the earth, we should be so[520] heavy that we could hardly move at all.

We read[530] in the newspaper that a plane has reached the wonder-ful[540] rate of over 600 miles an hour, but what[550] is a rate like this when thought of side by[560] side with the rate at which light moves? As for[570] movement to the north or to the south, to the[580] east or to the west, we know that our movement[590] can be judged only in relation to some other object[600] which is at rest or which can be said to[610] be moving at a given rate away from or towards[620] us. The earth itself is turning at a great rate[630] and we do not feel this move-ment of itself. We[640] can judge the movement of the earth only in relation[650] to some other object which is not moving with it.[660] We have probably all had the experience of not being[670] able to tell which way a train is moving at[680] night when we cannot see anything out of the windows.[690] We cannot tell which way we are moving or at[700] what rate we are moving except in relation to another[710] object which is not moving with us.

And so we[720] find that many of the common expressions of daily life[730] have no meaning in themselves and become real for us[740] only when considered in relation to some other fact or[750] object.   (751)

No. 17

When some time ago we were giving a little thought[10] to the strange nature of Time, we let ourselves take[20] some comfort from the certainty that at least we knew[30] that each day was made up of

144

24 hours.[40]   A day, we lightly stated, had in it just[50] 24 hours, never 23 and never 25.   But[60] were we right in thinking that we knew this to[70] be the case?   Perhaps not, for when the expert comes[80] along he informs us that a day lasts 48[90] hours and at the same time does not exist at[100] all.   We open our eyes a little wider with surprise[110] and ask: "How can such things be?"   And we are[120] given a quite simple reason.

As we all learned at[130] school, our earth is always turning away from the west,[140] and the nearer a place is to the east the[150] earlier is the hour of day-break at that place.[160]   If, for example, we were living in a country at[170] a point on the earth where the distance round the[180] world is as great as it can be, and we[190] were to leave that country and go to another country[200] which is, let us say, a little over one thousand[210] miles more distant from the˙ west (that is, a distance[220] of $\frac{1}{24}$ of the distance round the world)[230] we would find that day-break was an hour earlier[240] in our new home than it had been in our[250] old home.   If we moved only five hundred miles towards[260] the east we would find the difference to be only[270] half an hour, and if we moved only 50 miles[280] we would find the difference to be as little as[290] three minutes.   If we look at a table of "lighting[300] up" times we note that these times differ widely for[310] different parts of the same country.   But long, long ago,[320] before the present age with its planes and TV,[330] men found that any form of exchange between nations was[340] made very difficult when there was no order in the[350] method of stating the time in different parts of the[360] world.   So, to make it possible for anyone in any[370] part of the world to know just what time it[380] was in any other part of the world, the following[390] course was agreed upon.

Man had already "cut up" the[400] day into 24 hours, and he now agreed to[410] cut up the earth into 24 divisions—each division,[420] of course, measuring about one thousand miles at its widest[430] point. The time over the whole of each division was[440] to be the same, the time in each division differing[450] by just one hour from the time in the next[460] division.   We, therefore, have a system whereby the minutes and[470] the seconds are the same all over the world, but[480] the hour is one hour earlier for each division as[490] we move towards the east.

Now we will say that[500] in the "first" of these divisions New Year's Day begins.[510]   Hour by hour New Year's Day reaches and passes through[520] one of the 24 divisions until at the end[530] of 24 hours it is in the "last division."[540]   By that time the day is coming to an end[550] in the first division, and the second of January is[560] beginning.   But the last division, too, must have its full[570] day and

24 hours must pass before New Year's[580] Day really comes to an end and dies in the[590] last of the 24 divisions. The first of January[600] lives for 48 hours. But while the first of January[610] has been continuing its life in this way the[620] second of January has been moving round the world. The[630] first hour of the second of January reaches the last[640] division just as the 24th hour of the first[650] of January dies, and at the same moment the third[660] of January begins in the first division. And so we[670] are faced with the strange truth that while a day[680] lasts 48 hours there is between the first and[690] 3rd of January no break at all. People in one[700] country can hear "Five Hours Back" coming to them over[710] the air, hearing in the evening something that is happening[720] in the afternoon in another country. And the people of[730] that country can have the equally remarkable experience of hearing[740] "Five Hours Forward." They can hear the people of another[750] country "seeing the New Year in" while it is for[760] them the early evening of the last day of the[770] old year. And if we are covering a long distance[780] by ship we have the experience of finding that a[770] certain day can last only 23 hours or for[800] as long as 25 hours! (806)

No. 18

This is the story which my friend sometimes tells on[10] a long summer evening, as we sit together by the[20] open window, finding pleasure in the sweet clear air after[30] the still heat of the day.

"In those days I[40] was an even better walker than I am today,[50] and as you know I still very much like a[60] good, quick walk. Well, on that particular August morning I[70] set out quite early, before the day was too warm[80] for easy walking. I carried with me enough food to[90] meet my small needs and was therefore able to keep[100] away from towns of any kind. I was healthy in[110] the way that the young are healthy, and I walked[120] with quick easy steps, covering the first eight miles of[130] the road in just under two hours. But with the[140] increasing warmth of the day my rate fell little by[150] little, until in the full heat of the day I[160] found that I was doing very little more than two[170] and a half miles an hour. Even the small additional[180] weight of the food I was carrying troubled me, and[190] as it was by this time several hours since my[200] last meal it seemed reasonable that I should look out[210] for a place where I could rest and have a[220] meal in peace.

"After a time I reached a point[230] where the road comes very near to a small river,[240] and I was pleased enough by that time to walk[250] across the field and to find near the water some[260] undergrowth high enough to offer me some cover from[270] the full light and heat of the open countryside[280] round about. I took water from the clear, quick-running[290] river, and built a small fire upon some stones, and[300] so made my simple meal. Such was the heat of[310] the day that it was as much as I could[320] do to keep my eyes open, but, using all my[330] will-power, I was about to clear away the rest[340] of the food when I saw standing before me a[350] little old woman. So lined was her face that it[360] seemed to me there was no room left upon it[370] for any personal expression or feeling, and her dress was[380] as old as her face. Standing there, she appeared to[390] me to be not of this day, not of yesterday,[400] and not of tomorrow, but to represent Time itself.[410] But when she began to speak I found her words[420] were common-place enough.

"'Sir,' she said, 'Could you give[430] me some bread and perhaps some milk?'

"I immediately began[440] to clean up the piece of ground which had served[450] as a table for me, making a place for the[460] old woman to sit. I saw, however, that she took[470] almost nothing of the food and drink offered to her,[480] and as she sat without speaking I watched her face.[490]

"'Tell me, old woman,' I said, to my own complete[500] surprise, 'were you always as you are now or were[510] you once young and beautiful? Had you once a home[520] and a family, or have you always walked these roads[530] and fields?'

"The old woman turned her head and looked[540] at me for a long time without speaking. The lines[550] on her face grew even deeper, and her old blue[560] eyes were serious as she answered: 'Young man, I cannot[570] remember. For long ages I have walked these roads and[580] these fields. I have walked other roads and other fields.[590] Always I have walked and always I shall walk. I[600] am old, and perhaps I have never been young. I[610] am plain, and perhaps I have never been beautiful. But[620] you, you are young and you are beautiful. You are[630] strong and you have health. You have all the qualities[640] of the young. Because of these things I am speaking[650] to you now.'

"'Shall I tell her to go away?'[660] I thought. 'She does not know what she is talking[670] about anyway. I will stand up and get my things[680] together and continue my walk.'

"I moved, but immediately the[690] voice of this strange old woman came to me again.[700] 'No, do not go. You must hear what I have[710] to say.'

"'Yes,' I thought. 'I will wait and hear[720] what she has to say, for if she is as[730] wise as she is old her words may be of[740] some use to me in the future.'

"But the seconds[750] passed and no words came. I looked again and no[760] one was there. Not feeling very pleased with myself at[770] the thought that I must have been weak enough to[780] 'fall off' for a few minutes, and believing that these[790] things had not really happened, I began to clear up[800] what was left of my meal. And then I knew[810] that the old woman had been there, for my bread[820] was gone and in its place was this."

At this[830] point in his story my friend opens his hand, and[840] on it rests a lovely clear blue stone, in a[850] beautiful setting of gold.

"I always carry this about with[860] me now," he adds, "and I know that some day[870] I shall see that old woman again, and find out[880] what it was she had to say."   (887)

No. 19

It was a beautiful night. Although it was very warm[10] the air was clear, and it was possible to make[20] out the distant line of the higher land to the[30] east. The leaves moved a little as the night air[40] played among them, and we could hear the sounds of[50] the movement as we walked along.

The fireflies were out[60] in their hundreds, and their lights came and went as[70] they flew along. We could follow their course by watching[80] the coming and the going of their little lights. When[90] we first got out of the car and began to[100] walk we thought that everything was still and soundless, but[110] as we grew used to the night we found that[120] all was sound and movement. Masses of little living things[130] were on the move, and they all in turn gave[140] voice to their desires or needs as they went on[150] their way, perhaps looking for food, perhaps moving for no[160] reason at all except the desire not to be still.[170]

It was dangerous, people said, to walk about after night[180] had fallen. Animals were out under cover of the night,[190] and would not be seen until it was too late.[200] The great water-loving animals, who kept in the water[210] by day, came on land at night, and with their[220] great heavy bodies they could overturn a car. They could[230] run, too, and it would be very difficult for man[240] or woman to move quickly enough to get out of[250] their way once they charged.

"Just stories," we thought. "You[260] would not get these things happening so near to houses[270] and a town," we said. It was only a small[280] town, but still it was a town, and one did[290] not in these days get charged by animals in streets[300] and among houses.

But, of course, we were no longer[310] on the streets, and the lights of the nearest houses[320] could not be seen. The only lights we saw were[330] the little ones of the fireflies as they went on[340] their way, for purposes known only to themselves. It was[350] the kind of night on which anything could happen, for[360] not often in life are nights quite so perfect, quite[370] so cut off from all that is real and earthly.[380]

We made our way little by little to the water.[390] At last we came into the open, and there in[400] front of us was a mighty inland sea, a piece[410] of water two hundred miles and more across. The water[420] was still and was touched by little points of light[430] copied from the millions of white bodies over our heads.[440] They looked so near in that clear night that we[450] had the feeling that we could touch them if we[460] sailed on the waters.

"If only we had a little[470] sailing ship now!" we cried. "If only we could sail[480] away, out and out on this still, beautiful water."

"If[490] we sailed away now," said one, "I am sure we[500] could never come back. That water is not of this[510] world, I am sure, and when daylight came we should[520] find ourselves in the great unknown."

We did not really[530] believe this, and yet it seemed possible. Anything seemed possible[540] on such a night and in such a place. Then[550] we heard the strangest sound and, looking in its direction,[560] we saw—our eyes now used to the blackness—great[570] animals coming out of the water and on to the[580] land, about two hundred yards away.

Without speaking we turned[590] away, trying not to call attention to our movements. When[600] we were out of the open and among the undergrowth[610] once more we walked quickly. As we got near to[620] the car we said: "You see, those stories are not[630] true. The things keep near to the water. They would[640] not come all this way." But when we reached our[650] car we found it on its side, and the footmarks[660] of a large animal were clearly to be seen on[670] the earth nearby.

(673)

No. 20

The woman sat at the open window and looked out[10] upon the peaceful and well-known scene. It was June[20] and the countryside was looking its best. The leaves were[30] fully out but had not yet lost the sweet light[40] colours of the early summer months. The scene was indeed[50] beautiful because of its lovely colours, for the form of[60] the land itself was rather without interest. There were no[70] highlands and no lowlands to break up the great plain[80] which went on and on for many miles. The place[90] was dependent upon the little things to make it interesting[100] and pleasing to the eye, having no great land masses[110] to hold the eye and the attention.

All those little[120] details were well-known to the woman who watched from[130] her window on that June day. She knew just how[140] much growth had been added to the plants under her[150] window since June had last come and gone; she knew[160] just what would appear from each part of the ground[170] round the house, when to expect it, and how to[180] care for it. Her knowledge of the countryside and of[190] her own little piece of land had grown up naturally[200] within her during the 15 years that she had lived[210] in that old stone house. It was quite a small[220] house with two rooms looking out on to the road[230] and two bedrooms above. It was simple and plain but[240] it met her needs and the needs of her small[250] family. The first of her children, a boy, was at[260] school and another hour would pass before he would return,[270] running along the little road that led to the house.[280] The younger of her children was a little girl, and[290] the woman could see her at play from where she[300] sat. She was a happy, healthy-looking young girl of[310] 8, with the lovely natural colouring that results from good[320] food and enough of it, and good clean air.

While[330] the mother sat at the window she was not thinking[340] either of the loveliness of the countryside or of the[350] healthy colour in her children's faces. Those were the things[360] that were part of life itself and they were the[370] things in danger of being lost, lost for ever. If[380] once she and her little family left there they would[390] never return, of that she was certain. And it was[400] of that possible going away that she thought so seriously[410] as she sat by the little window on that peaceful[420] June day.

Father had been offered a good position in[430] the City and, while he said that he would do[440] whatever she wished in the matter, while he left it[450] to her to say yes or no, he desired very,[460] very much to take up the position, and she knew[470] that this was so. Nor did she think him wrong.[480] He had, she knew, a good, quick mind, a mind[490] that was never still, a mind ever at work on[500] some idea or another. On the long nights of the[510] long winters he would read his books and work out[520] ideas and plans, and in the mornings he would go[530] off to his work which made no demands at all[540] upon that clear mind. His voice was never heard speaking[550] against his work or his way of life, but because[560] she loved him she knew that deep inside him was[570] the desire for something more than that easy, peaceful life[580] gave him. A month ago two gentlemen from the big[590] city had called at his office in connexion with some[600] business and out of that call had come this offer[610] of employment at a rate of pay that would offer[620] them great advantages. There would be money for better education[630] for the children, which was a big consideration. On the[640] other hand, thought the woman, the good health of the[650] children might be lost if they lived near the city[660] with no fields to play in, no river by which[670] to fish, no well-known friends. Her brother's children were[680] very weakly and they had been brought up in a[690] big town. On and on went the thoughts. Father had[700] said that *she* must be the one to say yes[710] or no, but thinking of him she would have to[720] say yes. If, however, she told him that he must[730] be the one to say yes or no he would[740] think of her and say no. "I must begin to[750] sort our things out," she said. "Father must have his[760] opportunity. He has worked so hard for it." (768)

No. 21

The heat of the day had been such that even[10] the houses seemed to be on fire. If you put[20] out a hand to touch one of the old stones[30] of which the houses were built you took your hand[40] away quickly, feeling that it had been burned. The air[50] itself could be seen, never still but moving upwards from[60] the streets and the houses and the distant fields.

It[70] was not usual for the little town to be so[80] very warm. For some years past the summer had been[90] rather cold with poor weather, and the people kept to[100] their warm dresses and did not trouble to spend time[110] and money on buying light things which they might put[120] on perhaps once only in a year. Nature, however, has[130] her own little ways of interesting herself and us, and[140] she loves nothing better than to do something that is[150] not expected of her. To give us a very cold[160] day in January and a very warm one in August[170] is easy. There is no interest for Mother Nature in[180] that, and she loves to play with us, giving us[190] a warm December and a cold August. Still, if she[200] did that every year that, too, would become the expected,[210] so this year she has given the little town where[220] we live the warmest August on record. At first the[230] people loved it, and put up with their heavy winter[240] dress, but after several days they began to feel a[250] little weak.

"It is lovely," they said, "but of course[260] we are not used to it."

Less and less coverings[270] were placed on the beds at night, and the few[280] stores in the little town soon sold all their summer[290] dresses and wired to the wholesalers for more. The men[300] continued, of course, to put on each day their heavy[310] things for it is difficult for a man to change[320] his ways. Nearly all the men were employed in the[330] great new works that had been built just outside the[340] town shortly after the war. From the high ground about[350] two miles beyond the town you could see the sea[360] to the south, but the downs were between the town[370] and the sea, and no suggestion of sea air reached[380] the people as they went to and from their labour.[390] The air was heavy, and the people seemed to feel[400] its weight as they walked about. Plants were dying just[410] when they should have been at their best, and the[420] lovely colours were going from the countryside.

If you sat[430] at your door in the evening you could hear little[440] pieces of the talk going on among friends, for all[450] doors and windows were kept open until the last light[460] of day had gone.

"I shall die if it lasts[470] much longer," says a high young voice, a voice full[480] of health. "I shall just die."

"Die you will not,"[490] answers an old and rather weak voice. "Die you surely[500] will not just because of a little heat. Heat? Now[510] when *I* was your age . . ." and the story of those[520] past days is told, only to be followed by another[530] story from some still more aged person going back still[540] further into the past.

"What is the matter with you[550] all, to be sure?" asks a strong young man. "It[560] is a change from being cold, anyway."

Then from quite[570] nearby comes the sweet young voice of a girl talking[580] to a boy. "It would be lovely to see the[590] sea," she is saying. "Do you think it would be[600] worth the trouble of walking to the downs and looking[610] out at the sea? It must look so still and[620] peaceful and beautiful."

"I would walk to the end of[630] the world for you, Penny." "Even in this heat?" "Even[640] in this heat," he answered. Two people in the little[650] town found life to their liking. (656)

No. 22

I happened yesterday to hear on the radio the question:[10] "If you could be some other person who would you[20] want to be?" And the answer was: "Myself." At this[30] the first man asked again: "Why, what is so wonderful[40] about being you?" And this time the answer was: "There[50] is nothing so wonderful about it but it is very[60] comfortable."

All this was not, of course, meant to be[70] taken seriously, but I could not help thinking that really[80] it *is* comfortable to be just ourselves even though it[90] is not particularly wonderful.

The question: "Who would you like[100] to be?" is not a new one, and I am[110] sure all of us have played at times with the[120] idea of being some other person. If we are girls[130] or women we think at first, perhaps, that it would[140] be lovely to be a very, very beautiful person. Then[150] we think that perhaps it would be still better to[160] have masses and masses of money so that we could[170] buy whatever we desired at the moment we desired it.[180] We might perhaps think that it would be wonderful to[190] be able to marry the most good-looking man in[200] the world.

If it is a man thinking along these[210] lines he will probably want to be a person well[220] known in science or in the political field; he will[230] want to be a person well in the public eye.[240] He, too, might find the idea of having masses and[250] masses of money rather pleasing, but it is not very[260] likely that he will wish to be out-standingly good-looking.[270]

There is nothing particularly wrong about playing with the idea[280] of being very beautiful or very well-to-do or[290] well known because we all know at the same time[300] that "wishing will not make it so." There are indeed[310] some other words that we still hear from time to[320] time on the radio. They are: "Whatever will be will[330] be. The future is not ours to see. What will[340] be will be." The future certainly is not ours to[350] see, but there is one thing about the future that[360] is certain, and that is that we shall continue to[370] be ourselves and shall not get out of bed one[380] morning to find that we are some other person. And[390] this is just as well because we can be sure[400] that, however many troubles and difficulties we may have in[410] our lives, it is still much more comfortable to be[420] ourselves than to be another person. It would be very[430] strange indeed to get up one day and find everything[440] changed, to see everything with different eyes, to feel everything[450] with different hands, to think with a different mind, and[460] to have a different store of thoughts and memories. The[470] most serious of the changes would probably be to find[480] ourselves thinking with a different mind. If we have always[490] believed in telling the truth and in being kind to[500] others, we could find little pleasure in the mind of[510] a person who believed in reaching his or her own[520] end regardless of truth or kindness. If we have always[530] looked at the world with eyes that have found

153

Nature[540] beautiful and wonderful, it would be hard to find our-selves[550] without a moment in which to interest ourselves in the[560] daily movement and change round about us. Even less pleasing[570] is the idea of the loss of our own memories.[580] All the things, all the people and events we have[590] loved in the past, would be lost to us, and[600] we should find in our minds in place of them[610] another set of memories of people and events, and they[620] would certainly be of a different order from our own.[630]

Of course, you will say that these things would not[640] really matter because if we became another person we should[650] think and act as that person and we should like[660] it, having no memory at all of our old selves.[670] That, no doubt, is true but the important point is[680] that in wanting to be that other person we should[690] have to take all the other changes as well. We[700] could not just have the good looks or the money[710] or the good opinion of the world. It would be[720] all or nothing, and our personality would be lost to[730] us. In its place would be another and quite different[740] personality.

It seems a great comfort, therefore, to know that[750] we shall never have the opportunity to make such a[760] change. We shall go on just being ourselves.   (768)

No. 23

How we say a thing is generally just as important[10] as what we say. Sometimes it is important because we[20] can change the meaning of the words we use by[30] the way we say them. If we place weight on[40] one word rather than on another we can change the[50] "feeling" of our words. By changing the expression of our[60] voice we can suggest that we are serious or that[70] we are speaking only in play. For example, you may[80] say to a friend: "You really are the most senseless[90] person I ever met!" With such a remark you could[100] break with your friend for ever, but in 9 cases[110] out of 10 such a remark will have been made[120] lightly, as if in play, and if under the words[130] there is just a suggestion of seriousness your friend is[140] free not to remark upon it because you have made[150] the statement so lightly.

Sometimes people do not wish it[160] to be said that they are not speaking the truth,[170] and yet they do not want to speak the truth.[180] They therefore take words which in themselves could be true[190] but use them in such a way as to suggest[200] a different meaning.

It is not, however, only in connexion[210] with meaning or the results of our words that it[220] is important to be careful. How we use our voices[230] is important in itself. We often hear such remarks as:[240] "She has such a pleasing speaking voice" or "Her voice[250] really gets me down. I simply could not live with[260] it." And it is true that there are voices we[270] like to hear and voices that we do not like[280] to hear.

Few of us really know the sound of[290] our own voices. It seems that our hearing is not[300] planned in such a way as to let us hear[310] ourselves perfectly. We therefore often go through life thinking we[320] speak in one way when, in fact, we speak in[330] some quite different way. Our opportunities for hearing our own[340] voices are much better than they used to be because[350] recording machines are now quite common, and most of us[360] can find an opportunity at some time or another to[370] speak into such a machine and then have the record[380] played back. Generally such an experience is a surprise. I[390] was personally very much surprised at my own voice. The[400] first time I heard a record of it was some[410] years ago. I was in a strange town, and I[420] went into a big store. This store offered for quite[430] a small sum to let you speak into the recording[440] machine and they would then send the record of your[450] voice to any part of the world. I thought it[460] would be good to send a few words home to[470] my mother, and I accordingly thought up a few words,[480] said them, paid, and went away. Some weeks afterwards I[490] heard the record. It was a surprise but not just[500] the kind of surprise I like. I had always thought[510] I had a rather light voice and said my words[520] reasonably quickly. I found that on the record my voice[530] was low, almost deep, and that I had been speaking[540] at a very low rate.

More recently I made a[550] full-size record, speaking throughout at 100 words a[560] minute, but the result was just the same. On the[570] play-back I heard a low, rather deep voice, speaking[580] at about 10 words a minute!

We can never really[590] know ourselves—what we look like, what we sound like,[600] how our actions appear to others. Perhaps this is just[610] as well because, even if we cannot really see ourselves[620] as we are, it is equally certain that other people[630] do not see us as we really are, either. The[640] opinions each person holds about another person are influenced by[650] that person's many experiences, as well as by the quality[660] of the person's own hearing and seeing.

There is one[670] thing that we can do, however, and that is to[680] train ourselves to speak and act in a way that[690] we ourselves believe to be satisfactory. If we cannot please[700] others we can at least try to please ourselves, but[710] it is important, highly important in fact, that we try[720] to follow only the best examples. (720)

No. 24

Paper itself has come to us from the Far East[10] where it was first used, but the word *paper* has[20] come down to us from the Near East and different[30] forms of the word are found in several languages. Paper[40] is certainly one of the most common things in the[50] modern world. Every day masses of it are used; every[60] day masses of it are burnt; and every day masses[70] more of it are made and supplied to the waiting[80] people of the world.

People always want paper and the[90] manufacturer of it need not fear that the demand for[100] his product will fall off. Without paper our modern life[110] would, at least for a time, come to a complete[120] stop. It is indeed very much to be questioned whether[130] our modern life could ever have come about had there[140] been no paper or some other product of a like[150] nature which was cheap, lasting, and serviceable.

Without paper we[160] could not write letters to one another. Millions of letters[170] are written every day, some very important and some of[180] little importance, and they are all written on paper. Before[190] the use of paper, writing had first to be done[200] by cutting the characters out of stone and later by[210] using materials which cost so much that only such people[220] as Kings and army leaders could have them. The common[230] people could not write and it would have been useless[240] had they been able to write because there would have[250] been nothing on which to write. And, of course, we[260] can see at once how impossible it would be to[270] teach people to write if there was no cheap material[280] on which to write.

Today, we in this country all[290] go to school as children and there we learn to[300] write and to read, and as soon as we can[310] write and read simple words we begin to learn other[320] things until most of us end up by knowing something[330] about quite a number of things. Some know more and[340] some know rather less, but it is just about impossible[350] to find anyone in this country today who has not[360] had the opportunity to learn. And for this happy state[370] of things we generally thank the Government. Little more than[380] a hundred years ago it was by no means a[390] natural thing for all children to go to school; but[400] the Governments that have followed one another throughout the years[410] have made it more and more possible for young people[420] to go to school until we have reached the state[430] today when we believe that not only should all children[440] go to school and so learn to read and to[450] write, but we believe further that all children should be[460] given the opportunity to receive higher education if they show[470] themselves able to take advantage of such training.

The Governments[480] have been very wise and helpful in passing all the[490] Acts which have brought us to this happy state, but[500] the fact is that it was really the supply of[510] cheap paper in great amounts that made it possible for[520] us all to learn. Can we picture what school life[530] would be like without our notebooks and our instruction books?[540] There would stand a teacher and facing him would sit[550] 20, 30, or 40 little children longing, let us say,[560] to read and to write, to learn about the history[570] of their own country and of other countries, to learn[580] about their own land and about other lands. But the[590] teacher has no books because he has no paper, and[600] the children have nothing on which they can write and[610] then take away their work and learn it. Everything must[620] be done from memory. The teacher has to remember what[630] he has been told and the children in their turn[640] have to remember what they have been told. Memory is[650] often a poor help. Nearly everyone finds it easier to[660] learn through reading words than through hearing them. If we[670] wish we can read the words in a book over[680] and over again but the words of the teacher, once[690] said, are lost for ever. We can, of course, ask[700] him to say them over again, but the time taken[710] to learn wholly in this way would be so great[720] that the children would end up by knowing very little[730] in most cases.

Learning became general when books became general.[740] While books were the property of the few, learning was[750] also the property of the few. Now books may be[760] had for the asking and learning, too, may be had[770] for the asking. It is only our personal qualities that[780] limit the field of our knowledge.

(786)

No. 25

Do you take an interest in life? You might well[10] answer that it all depends upon what "taking an interest"[20] means, and you would do well to answer in that[30] way because much trouble is caused in life through people[40] not expressing themselves in a clear enough way. If by[50] "taking an interest in life" is meant that we would[60] rather be living than dying, it is probable that almost[70] every living person is interested.

If, however, we take it[80] as given that everyone would rather live than die, we[90] must find other meanings for the words. We can indeed[100] be interested in life from very many points of view.[110] Many well-to-do and highly successful business men have[120] reached that happy state because they have found a great[130] interest in living their own lives to the full and[140] not paying too much attention to other people's actions. They[150] have got up each day ready to overcome any difficulties[160] that may face them and willing to meet any demands[170] that life may make upon them. When times have been[180] bad they have not lost hope; when times have been[190] good they have not lost their heads but have remembered[200] that the years in front of them might not always[210] be so good. They have given of their best in[220] their daily lives, and in return they have found success.[230]

It is not everyone, however, who can find working life[240] so satisfactory in itself. It is not everyone who can[250] find work that meets all the needs of the mind.[260] Such people demand pleasures beyond those of labour, and they[270] try to find an interest in life in other directions.[280] But the directions are so many that it is not[290] easy to know in which direction to look. Happily, we[300] do not as a rule have to look far for[310] we seem to have natural interests. It seems to come[320] quite naturally to us to sort out our feelings, and[330] from the great number of possible fields of interest we[340] find forces pulling us this way or that.

The interests[350] of some people change considerably with the passing of the[360] years; other people seem to hold an interest in the[370] same kind of things throughout their whole lives. Some people,[380] for example, have a life-long interest in getting together[390] sets of books, particularly copies of the first publication of[400] a book. Others like to buy pictures, and they always[410] hope that one day they will have the pleasure of[420] buying an old picture very cheaply only to be told[430] afterwards by the experts that it is a true Old[440] Master and is worth many thousands of pounds. Such finds[450] were certainly possible in times past, but it is doubtful[460] whether in these days there are many Old Masters which[470] have been put away and which no one has afterwards[480] remembered, so that they are now just waiting for the[490] day when an expert will discover their true worth. Too[500] many people have for too long been finding an interest[510] in the buying and selling of pictures to make it[520] possible for such an event to happen often. Still, people[530] go on hoping and quite rightly so. With books there[540] may be the same hope: one day a person may[550] have the happiness of buying an old second hand-book[560] for a few pennies only to discover afterwards that it[570] is a very valuable book indeed, and would get a[580] high price if offered for sale.

There are people who[590] have a deep interest in show business of all kinds,[600] serious or otherwise. Some people find their interest

158

in the[610] open air life, and they are never so happy as[620] when walking over the downs or through the fields; or[630] perhaps their love for the open air leads them to[640] take a very great interest in the large or small[650] piece of land round their house. It must be kept[660] perfect, they feel, and very lovely such places generally look.[670] There are many persons, young ones particularly, who find much[680] pleasure in playing records. They will sit beside their record[690] player for hours, playing over the most recent records they[700] have bought.

For some people "taking an interest in life"[710] means keeping up-to-date in their knowledge of passing[720] events. They read books and newspapers which keep them informed[730] about the most recent developments in science or in the[740] political field, and in industry or engineering. At all costs[750] they wish to be well informed on daily events.

Whatever[760] form our interest may take, it is important to have[770] such an interest. (773)

No. 26

It was just a day at the office like any[10] other. Being there first, as she nearly always was, Penny[20] took the cover off her machine and gave the machine[30] a quick clean. This did not take long because Penny[40] did it each day, and the machine was, therefore, kept[50] in very good condition. From time to time she oiled[60] it as well, and because of these kind attentions the[70] machine caused her no trouble.

She then cleaned Mr. White's[80] table, making quite sure that everything was ready and in[90] order. Mr. White was quite a good employer and easy[100] to work with, as a rule, but he did sometimes[110] make a scene if small things went wrong. So Penny[120] had found out that the best thing to do was[130] to make sure that nothing went wrong.

By the time[140] all these small matters had been seen to, Miss West[150] had come in. Penny and Miss West both worked for[160] Mr. White. Penny was only 17 years of age and[170] had been in the office for less than a year,[180] whereas Miss West was 22 and had been with[190] Mr. White for 4 years. Penny did not mind being[200] under Miss West because she knew that she had not[210] yet had enough experience to take the full responsibility herself,[220] and moreover Miss West was almost always kind and helpful.[230] Of course, if Mr. White made life difficult for Miss²⁴⁰ West for any reason, she then passed it on and²⁵⁰ made things difficult for Penny, but on the whole all²⁶⁰ was quite peaceful and such upsets did not last long.²⁷⁰

Miss West opened her notebook and began to complete letters²⁸⁰ left over from the day before, while Penny put answered²⁹⁰ letters away and placed copies of letters sent out into³⁰⁰ the Letter Book. They worked without speaking for about half³¹⁰ an hour. Then the door opened once again and Mr.³²⁰ White passed through the office on the way to his³³⁰ own room, which opened out of the general office.

He³⁴⁰ was a small man with quick movements, a man who³⁵⁰ seemed to be able to get through a great amount³⁶⁰ of work in no time at all. He seemed, too,³⁷⁰ to remember the smallest details of everything that had happened.³⁸⁰ He remembered the names of all of his customers, and³⁹⁰ he always considered their personalities when writing or speaking to⁴⁰⁰ them. He often used to remark that it was not⁴¹⁰ only the quality of a product that made it easy⁴²⁰ to sell a thing: it was also an understanding of⁴³⁰ the person to whom the goods were to be sold.⁴⁴⁰ If the customer liked you and believed that you liked⁴⁵⁰ him, he used to say, the sale was already half-⁴⁶⁰way towards being made.

Having read through the morning's letters⁴⁷⁰—which he liked to open himself—Mr. White called Miss⁴⁸⁰ West into his office to take down some answers. Penny⁴⁹⁰ went off, as she did each morning during the winter⁵⁰⁰ months, to heat up some milk. She took this in⁵¹⁰ for Mr. White and Miss West. Often, however, Miss West's⁵²⁰ milk went cold because, as she said: "He never stops⁵³⁰ speaking for long enough for me to touch it!" In⁵⁴⁰ the summer months, of course, the morning drink was something⁵⁵⁰ very cold, and Miss West's trouble was that it became⁵⁶⁰ warm before she could touch it!

And so the events⁵⁷⁰ of the day were much as they always were. As⁵⁸⁰ it was a Wednesday, however, Penny went out at 12.30⁵⁹⁰ to a little place near to the office where⁶⁰⁰ the meals were rather better than at most places which⁶¹⁰ were within her means. The meal cost a little more⁶²⁰ than on other days of the week but she went⁶³⁰ there happily because six girls of her own age and⁶⁴⁰ from her old school met there each Wednesday to have⁶⁵⁰ a meal together and to exchange news and views. Penny⁶⁶⁰ looked forward to these Wednesday meetings very much. The girls⁶⁷⁰ talked freely of any difficulties they met with in their⁶⁸⁰ work, and she was able to learn more about office⁶⁹⁰ life in this way than would have been possible in⁷⁰⁰ one small office.   (703)

160

No. 27

Time, as we have remarked before, is the most valuable[10] thing that we have to spend. We can use our[20] time or we can waste it, just as we can[30] use or waste our money. There is one very important[40] difference between time and money, however. All the people who[50] are reading these words own different amounts of money: no[60] two people, in all probability, would be found to have[70] just the same sum, down to the last penny, if[80] all the money to which they had a right were[90] put down on the table. But everyone has the[100] same amount of time. We all have our 24[110] hours each day, and for everyone of us the[120] hour will supply just sixty minutes of time, no more[130] and no less. The minute will give us sixty seconds,[140] no more and no less, and there is nothing whatever[150] that we can do about it, try as we may.[160] Sometimes we long to make time pass more quickly because[170] we are waiting for something wonderful to happen, and sometimes[180] we long to make the time pass less quickly because[190] we like the present moment so much. Science, which has[200] done such wonderful things, has not yet found a way[210] to change this regular passing of time.

It does not[220] seem certain, however, that time is really quite the same[230] for everyone of us. It is true that we[240] cannot get away from the seconds, minutes and hours of[250] each day, but it is possible that some people have[260] a feeling for time which is different from that of[270] other people. This may account for the fact that there[280] are people who seem to be able to get through[290] a great amount of work in quite a short time[300] while there are others who, no matter how hard they[310] work, seem to get very little done. This is not[320] the result of any real difference in time itself, however:[330] it is probably owing to a difference in the way[340] that our minds work. If one person has a mind[350] that is very quick, that sees the point of some[360] remark at once, that knows the answer to a question[370] almost before the question has been asked—then that person[380] is certainly likely to do more in any given time[390] than the person who needs to look this way and[400] that before seeing the point of a remark, and who[410] has to think hard and long before being able to[420] answer a question. That is a difference in the mind,[430] not in the passing of time.

Much of our time[440] is spent at work, in school, office or home, but[450] it is a poor day that offers us no time[460] at all to spend how we like, and the way[470] we spend those few hours that we have to ourselves[480] differs from person to person. In these days quite a[490] considerable part of people's free time is spent in watching[500] TV. Before the coming of TV people spent[510] more time with the radio.

Before the radio came there[520] were the "pictures," and before that there were books.[530] All these ways of spending time now exist together, and[540] we have many ways of keeping ourselves interested.

It has[550] always been considered respectable to read books. Even when a[560] person spent rather too much time upon reading, sitting up[570] at night when he should have been in bed, he[580] was in some way respected for this. To read was[590] to learn and to get knowledge was a good thing.[600] But, of course, many people did not read to learn.[610] Many read light books—love stories, for example—and when[620] young people read such stories their mothers would say that[630] they were wasting time and that "they" did not read[640] such things when "they" were young. When it came to[650] "going to the pictures" the pictures were not considered quite[660] respectable. It was perhaps all right to go to the[670] pictures, say, once a week but to go more often[680] was somehow not quite the thing, and when young people[690] did anything wrong it was put down to the bad[700] influence of the pictures. The possible bad influence of light[710] reading was no longer remembered, and the old people of[720] the new day would say that "they" did not go[730] to the pictures in "their" young days.

Today it is[740] the turn of TV. Watching TV night after[750] night is often said to be the cause of wrong[760] acts committed by young people because, of course, the old[770] people of the still newer age did not watch TV[780] in "their" young days.

Perhaps a form of pleasure[790] has to be more or less out-of-date before[800] we can consider it a respectable way of passing the[810] time?   (811)

No. 28

The young woman walked from room to room of the[10] house. It was not a very large house; it was,[20] indeed, a house like so many others up and down[30] the country. It had in it 5 rooms, two down[40] with 3 bedrooms above. It had electric fires in all[50] the bedrooms and an electric water-heating system.

The fact[60] that her house was just like thousands of other small[70] houses did not influence the judgment of the young woman[80] at all. In one way it was quite different from[90] all the other houses, for it was hers. It was[100] her own house to live in and to make comfortable[110] and beautiful. It was her own house, and she had[120] made up her mind to live happily in it and[130] to make all who lived in it happy as well.[140]

162

Her mind was serious as she moved about, but her[150] heart was light. "I am a married woman now," she[160] thought. "I am a married woman with all the responsibility[170] that goes with marriage, but how happy I am!"

And,[180] of course, she ought to have been happy. Her name[190] was Penny. Two weeks before she had been Penny Wills:[200] now she was Penny Read, and had been married for[210] two weeks. Only the day before she had returned from[220] the seaside to begin her life in her new home.[230]

The house itself was not new but it was quite[240] modern, and she had spent much time during the last[250] few weeks buying materials and making up her mind about[260] colours. The paint work she had kept light in colour,[270] but in each room she had employed a different basic[280] colour. One room, for example, was light blue while another[290] was done in a very, very light golden colour. The[300] paint in the sitting-room and in the best bedroom[310] was, however, white. It was all very pleasing, even to[320] the eye of a person not particularly interested, and to[330] Penny it was just wonderful.

She had received many presents,[340] for she was a girl with an agreeable nature and[350] many friends, and those presents she was now putting out,[360] taking care that each thing should go in the best[370] possible place for it. She had received six pictures and[380] each picture had to be placed in such a way[390] that it showed to the best advantage. She did not[400] want a picture where so little light fell on it[410] that it could not be seen clearly; but, on the[420] other hand, she did not want the full light to[430] fall on it in such a way that no one[440] could see the picture. Every detail was important to Penny[450] as she carried on with her happy work, and she[460] did everything with loving care.

Before her work had come[470] to an end, however, she had to leave it and[480] to think of food. Her special friend was calling on[490] her that afternoon. It would be the first time in[500] her life that she had had a friend call on[510] her in her own home, and it was quite, quite[520] necessary that everything should be perfect. She had been trained[530] in the arts of housekeeping, and it was not long[540] before all sorts of good things were ready. To set[550] the table for two was a small matter, but even[560] that seemed to take a long time, so carefully was[570] it done. Then Penny had to change her dress. The[580] dress she had on was pleasing enough but it was[590] not new. Her friend had already seen it. Penny believed[600] that as a married woman she ought to put on[610] a new dress so that she would look just as[620] different in the eyes of her friend as she was[630] feeling in her own heart. (635)

Today we have so many different means of getting comfortably[10] and quickly from one place to another that we perhaps[20] do not value some of these means as much as[30] we ought. In the early days of man's development he[40] had to walk or to run if he desired to[50] get from one place to another. Then, after many years,[60] he discovered that he could sit on the back of[70] an animal if he moved on land, and in this[80] way he sat at ease while the animal laboured for[90] him. The animal used naturally differed in different countries. A[100] very important development came when men discovered that they could[110] move across water. The object that carried them over the[120] water in those far-off days could not be called[130] a ship as we understand that word today. Poor as[140] the methods may have been, however, they did let men[150] reach places that would be otherwise cut off by water.[160] For thousands of years there was no development beyond this.[170] There existed no quick means of movement. Life was simple[180] and hard.

But things do not stand still. We must,[190] we are told, move onwards or move back, and men[200] seem always to have desired to move forward. No matter[210] what point they reach, they always see something more calling[220] them onwards. Out of this desire for a better material[230] life came good roads, big ships, railways, motor-cars and[240] planes. So used are we to wonderful planes and to[250] powerful motor-cars that we are in danger of under-[260]valuing the railway, that rather out-of-date method of[270] moving across the country! Few people in these days use[280] the railway for pleasure: they use it because it is[290] a useful means of getting somewhere reasonably quickly. If a[300] friend tells us that he is going somewhere by plane[310] we are immediately interested. If he tells us that he[320] has bought a handsome new car and is going to[330] such and such a place we are likely to be[340] interested. If he is going overseas in one of the[350] large and modern ships all his friends will want to[360] see him off. Let him go by rail, however, and[370] no one will take the smallest interest in him. Railways[380] are all right in their way, but they are not[390] "news"!

Yet the railway has played an important part in[400] the greatness of our country. Railways have quite a long[410] history if we go back to the times when the[420] trains were led by horses, but they have a history[430] of only a hundred or so years when we speak[440] of the railway in its modern form. The present heavy[450] railway, with great engines and iron or steel railway lines,[460] was developed in this country, and from here it was[470] soon sent to most parts of the world. The English-[480]built railways were found not only in this country but[490] in other countries overseas, and in a remarkably short time[500] engines were carrying trains full of people and goods at[510] rates as high as those used today.

These rates do[520] not seem very remarkable today, used as we are to[530] hearing of planes moving at 500 or a thousand[540] miles an hour, but they seemed very remarkable to people[550] a hundred years ago. There were no motor-cars and[560] the horse was used as the quickest, safest and best[570] means of getting about on roads that were for the[580] most part very bad indeed. Quite small distances often took[590] days to cover. In such conditions as these it is[600] natural that the railway seemed a thing of most outstanding[610] importance. It is certain that without it this country could[620] not have gone forward in the wonderful way it has.[630] It is doubtful whether even the plane in this age[640] has really been so important for the country as the[650] train was in the earlier age. In the building of[660] railways this country led the world, but in recent years[670] certain other countries have shown more drive in keeping their[680] railways clean and up-to-date. (686)

No. 30

Sometimes it seems that the more we know and the[10] more we learn, the less remarkable we consider our learning[20] and our knowledge to be. When other people can do[30] something that we ourselves cannot do we think that those[40] people must be very wonderful indeed; we think that they[50] must be of much more worth than we ourselves are.[60] Yet, as soon as we can do that same thing[70] we think nothing of it, and begin to look round[80] for something new to learn or to do.

It even[90] seems that we act in this same way in our[100] thoughts about the new goods and the new machines that[110] are so often and so readily put before us in[120] these days. It is, perhaps, difficult to continue to find[130] each new thing so very remarkable when new and better[140] things follow one another at such a great rate. We[150] still find ourselves greatly interested, however, when something quite new[160] comes along. The first plane to fly over water looks[170] a very poor thing if we see it now, but[180] it certainly caused more talk and general interest than the[190] largest and most modern plane causes today, let it have[200] four engines or eight engines, or as many as the[210] engineers wish. Planes are no longer new, and they are[220] hardly even news. The public expects its engineers and its[230] men of science to bring out newer and larger and[240] better planes. For what does the public pay taxes, if[250] not for such things, one might ask?

The first man-[260]made object to free itself from the earth's pull and[270] to fly off to the outer distances may be worth[280] several lines in the newspaper. The second such object may[290] be much bigger and it may leave the earth much[300] more quickly, but because it is not the first it[310] cannot hope to get the interest of the public in[320] the same way.

In these days we have the most[330] wonderful machines to do for us addition, division and other[340] sums. A thousand sums in a second is nothing to[350] such a machine. Quickly and still more quickly the figures[360] fly, but the public hardly cares. It is probable that[370] there was much more interest three hundred years ago in[380] the first adding machine ever made. That first machine was[390] made by a young man in the attempt to lessen[400] the labours of his father, who was responsible for taxation[410] and who worked long hours adding up figures. Further machines[420] followed, and it is interesting to note that all those[430] early machines were made by people working by themselves, all[440] on their own. In these days the usual thing is[450] for organized workers to act together in such matters.

The[460] first machine could work only addition or "take away" sums,[470] but in a few years a machine was made that[480] could be used for division and that represented a most[490] important step in the development of such machines.

The quick[500] development of this country during the Machine Age, a hundred[510] or more years ago, brought with it a growing demand[520] for adding machines. Business and industrial growth took place side[530] by side with the growth in the size of the[540] banks and the increased use of the credit system. It[550] was natural that the time soon came when most banks[560] and offices could not think of operating without the help[570] of adding machines.

Now we have machines that can do[580] the most surprising and difficult pieces of work. Difficult sums[590] that might take a man a year or more to[600] do are carried out in a matter of minutes. If[610] the machine goes wrong it knows that it has done[620] so, and it takes action to put things right. These[630] machines are said to have a memory; they are even[640] said by some to think. In fact, some man somewhere[650] has to do the thinking first, and the machine acts[660] afterwards according to that man's instructions. It cannot act by[670] itself but can do only what it is told to[680] do. It cannot, therefore, be said to have a mind[690] and to be able to think. The machine can, however,[700] store facts and figures and make use of them later,[710] and in that way it perhaps can be said to[720] have a memory. The machines are certainly wonderful but in[730] our daily lives we hardly give them a thought. They[740] represent just one of so many remarkable things, after all.

(750)

No. 31

If a book is really successful the public may buy[10] it in very large numbers. Sometimes we see figures showing[20] that several hundred thousand copies of a book have been[30] bought. It is of interest to ask: "What does the[40] public ask for in the books which it reads for[50] pleasure?" In this field, as with all other arts, there[60] is the man or the woman who says: "I do[70] not know much about writing, but I do know what[80] books I like to read." And if we may judge[90] from the books which have been great successes it seems[100] safe to say that what the masses of the people[110] ask for in their reading is a book which tells[120] a good story about interesting people, a book with movement[130] and life in it. There are always people ready to[140] give the public what it asks for in such respects,[150] and writers who wish to make money from their writing[160] have been almost forced to write books of the kind[170] which please the people who make up the largest market[180] for their work.

Now a book written with this public[190] in view may still be a good book, but very[200] often it is not the book which the writer would[210] have written had he been quite free to follow his[220] own wishes. The form of book provided by many writers[230] is the book which tells a clear story, which gives[240] a picture of a number of men and women who[250] at the beginning of the book are in one set[260] of conditions, and who move step by step throughout the[270] book into a different and more pleasing set of conditions.[280] Such a book gives the reader a sense of order.[290] The people in these books act and think along certain[300] lines, and it is only in details that the stories[310] differ.

But during recent years the more thoughtful writers have[320] been attempting a new form. It is said that the[330] course which our lives take depends upon our personal thoughts,[340] the thoughts which, if told at all, are told only[350] to those nearest or dearest to us. It is in[360] these personal thoughts that the writers are interested. The important[370] thing, they say, is to set down the life which[380] goes on in a man's mind—not so much the[390] thoughts which result from the day-to-day happenings, but[400] the long line of thoughts which

167

makes up his real[410] life. But both the old and the new form of[420] book are subject to material considerations, and it is not[430] possible for every event or every thought to be set[440] down.

All writers have to face this question of what[450] to use and what to leave out. The writer of[460] the book with a story uses those events or thoughts[470] which help on the telling of his story. The wish[480] of the writer of the new form of book is[490] to give a complete picture of the minds of the[500] people he is telling us about. So he makes his[510] book, or each part of his book, cover only a[520] short time, and gives a complete picture of what is[530] happening in the minds of the people during that time.[540] This new form is not always pleasing to readers used[550] only to the old form, as there are no clear[560] steps in the story told, and there is nothing final[570] at the end of the book. But while a reader[580] may find pleasure in reading a book which shows for[590] the hundredth time that two and two make four, it[600] is doubtful if he reads through three or four hundred[610] pages for that purpose. Without doubt he finds pleasure in[620] the book line by line and page by page. The[630] story is not a really necessary part of his pleasure[640] in reading, and it is probably that with the development[650] of the new form the general reader may come to[660] like it more.   (663)

No. 32

"Oh, for the good old days!" How often have we[10] heard those words! How often have we been told of[20] those good old days and of how happy they were.[30] In those days the weather during all the months of[40] the summer was perfect; in the winter it was just[50] what winter weather should be. Life was more peaceful; events[60] did not follow one another quite so quickly; friends were[70] more true and more understanding. There was more respect for[80] family life, men were happy in their work, and life[90] was a very good thing. Those past days, we are[100] told, were very different from the present days of restlessness[110] and doubt, of the wrong weather in both summer and[120] winter. Perhaps we ask: "When were those happy times, when[130] all men were brothers, and life was so easy and[140] free?" Some will answer that they were the years before[150] World War I. Others will place them round about 1900,[160] while others will place them in the "90's."

In [170] our reading also we come upon stories of the golden[180] days of the past, but we find here that at[190] all times during the past two thousand years men have[200] been pointing back to the happy days of old, attempting[210] to paint for us a picture of those happy days,[220] and to show us how much better those days were[230] than the times in which they were then living.

What[240] is the reason for this looking back into the past[250] to find happiness? Perhaps it is that at almost any[260] time there are many people who are leading happy lives[270] but who do not talk or write about it; but[280] there are also many others who were happy in their[290] young days but who have not changed with the ever-[300] changing conditions of the life going on about them. For[310] these people the world used to be a better place[320] than it is at present. There are few of us[330] who cannot look into the past and find happy days.[340]   As children, we have little or no control over the[350] details of our lives, but we are generally happy because[360] we are able more easily not to regard these details[370] if they do not please us.   We can cut ourselves[380] off from the outside world and build up a happy[390] world of our own.

It might be easy for us[400] to believe these people who find good only in the[410] conditions of the past were it not for the fact[420] that these same people will, at other times, tell us[430] how different things were when they were young, how hard[440] they were forced to work, for what long hours they[450] were kept at their work, how few pleasures they had,[460] and so on.   And for every book which we read[470] telling us of the good old days there will be[480] another telling us of the bad old days, of the[490] hard lives of the masses of the people.   Most of[500] us would not be willing to return to the conditions[510] of life as it was lived 30, 40 or 50[520] years ago.   We believe that it is better to be[530] living in the present, with all the troubles of the[540] present day.   We know that we have no right to[550] expect to be happy all the time, and we know[560] also that by keeping in touch with the life and[570] the thought and the interests of our own times, we[580] can help to make the present days happy ones, both[590] for ourselves and for others.

We can be certain, too,[600] that at some time in the future old people will[610] look back to these present days and will speak of[620] them as the "good old days."

(626)

No. 33

There are few of us who do not find pleasure[10] in the knowledge that we hold in our hands a[20] new book, and that we have before us the necessary[30] hour of rest and peace in which to read it.[40]   As we open the book what do we hope to[50] find in its pages? Are we hoping to increase our[60] knowledge of some particular subject? Are we expecting to find[70] beauty in the language of the book and in the[80] writer's expression of his thoughts? Or are we going to[90] read the book simply for the pleasure to be found[100] in the story which it will tell?

Some of us[110] will hope to find one thing and others will hope[120] to find a different thing. But if we are reading[130] just for the story, what kind of story do we[140] hope the book will tell? What do we wish the[150] book to give us? Do we want the story to[160] put before us a picture of life as it is,[170] showing us its dangers as well as its comforts, its[180] troubles as well as its happiness? Or do we want[190] the story to take us away from the real world[200] and to open out for us a world of the[210] "make-believe," to show us life as it might be[220] if this world were perfect, or as it might be[230] in a quite different world which exists only in the[240] mind of the writer? Our answers to these questions will[250] depend partly upon the state of our minds at the[260] time of the question being asked and partly upon the[270] general purpose of our reading. If we read with no[280] set purpose in mind we shall probably like best the[290] books of the second kind: if we are reading because[300] we regard the art of writing as something valuable in[310] itself, because we love to read well-written matter, because[320] we value expression of thought and idea, then we shall[330] probably want to read books of the first kind, the[340] books which attempt to paint a picture of life as[350] it is lived, day by day, by people in different[360] countries and in different stations of life. Books of this[370] kind are very often well-written, for it is the[380] writer with the most power over words who can most[390] successfully put before us these living pictures so that as[400] we read we say: "Yes, that is so. I have[410] seen that; I have experienced that." The writer is writing[420] of what he knows and of what he has seen.[430] Such books develop our minds, help us to think clearly,[440] and add to our own experience the experience of the[450] writer.

Many years ago a very well-known writer of[460] the time said that there were two kinds of book,[470] the books of the hour and the books of all[480] time. The difference, he continued, was not one of quality[490] only—it was not merely that the good book would[500] last while the bad book would not. It was a[510] difference of *kind*, for there were good books for the[520] hour and good books for all time, bad books for[530] the hour and bad books for all time. The book[540] of the make-believe world is generally a book of[550] the hour; it gives us pleasure while we read, but[560] once it has been read it is not long remembered.[570] Whether it is a good or a bad book depends[580] upon the quality of the mind of the writer and[590] whether or not he has something of value to say.[600] On the other hand, we may keep in our minds[610] for ever the memory of a book which shows us[620] the real world, but this is only possible if, again,[630] the writer has had something of value to say and[640] has expressed his thoughts in language which in itself gives[650] us pleasure.

The reading public grows yearly and the number[660] of books issued grows yearly. Which of last year's books[670] will still be read in the years to come? Few[680] of us would care to express an opinion.

(688)

No. 34

I want to talk for a little while this week[10] about shorthand writing. How many words a minute can you[20] write at present? How many words a minute would you[30] like to be able to write? Are you taking any[40] steps to increase your present rate of writing? I think[50] that there are very few of us who do not[60] feel that we would like to be able to write[70] more quickly: whether we can take down good shorthand notes[80] at 50 words a minute or at 250[90] words a minute, there is always present a desire[100] to add another 10, 20 or 50 words to our[110] rate of writing. I think also that it is probably[120] true to say that very few people ever reach the[130] highest rate at which they could write. I believe that[140] most writers could, with a little training and work, write[150] more quickly.

A question often asked is: "What rate of[160] writing is required to meet the needs of most office[170] workers?" Often you will find that the answer given is[180] to the effect that 80 words a minute will be[190] good enough to carry the writer through most of his[200] daily work. But experience has shown that in many offices[210] this is not the case, and I think that those[220] of you who are at present writing at 50 or[230] 80 words a minute should make up your minds that[240] you will continue your training until you can write at[250] 120 words a minute or over. If,[260] when you leave your day school, you are able to[270] write at 80, make up your minds to use a[280] little of your free time each week in perfecting your[290] knowledge of the system and in increasing your rate of[300] writing. You will not find it a waste of time[310] to do this. The good situations in offices are given[320] to those who can do better than the masses.

There[330] is, too, the question of your finding happiness in your[340] work. If, when you get out of bed each morning,[350] you know that you are going into an office where[360] you will be asked to do just a little more[370] than you are able to do, you will not feel[380] very happy about it. You will perhaps feel like the[390] little girl who was five years old and had been[400] at school for three weeks. She was asked by her[410] mother: "Well, and how do you like school?" "Oh," said[420] the little girl, "I wish I was married and out[430] of it all." If you take a real interest in[440] your work and know that you can easily meet the[450] demands which will be made upon you, then you are[460] likely to find happiness in it. Therefore, it is time[470] well used in your early days if you work hard[480] to become an expert writer. When you reach a rate[490] of 80 words a minute, do not regard it as[500] the end of the shorthand road, but rather as a[510] step on the road. Happily, our system of shorthand is[520] such that it is very easy to reach 120[530] and 140 words a minute,[540] and with a little work much higher rates can be[550] reached.

A few points for you to note are: Always[560] use good quality paper for your shorthand notes. Write lightly,[570] passing quickly from one outline to the next and from[580] the end of one line to the beginning of the[590] next. A light and easy touch is a sure way[600] to increase the rate of writing. Make sure that you[610] have a good knowledge of the general rules of the[620] system and of the special Short Forms. Read and copy[630] as much well-written shorthand as possible. While taking down[640] do not think of other things: think only of the[650] words being read out and of the outlines you are[660] writing.

Once you know the outline for a word or[670] a set of words, there is no reason why you[680] should not write that outline as quickly as the expert[690] writer.   (691)

No. 35

A little while ago we considered the rather strange fact[10] that it is very often the people who talk most[20] about the "good old days" who at other times tell[30] us about the very hard times they had in their[40] own early days. In these easy-going days, they say, young[50] people do not know what it is to work really[60] hard, and, they continue, it is as a direct result[70] of their own hard work that they are today[80] the men they are. And we, of course, are left[90] in no doubt whatever that we of the present day[100] can never hope to be as good men and women[110] as our fathers and mothers.

If this is the case,[120] the country today is in a very bad way.[130] But is it the case? If the young people of[140] today are of poorer quality than their fathers and[150] mothers, we may ask whether the old people of today[160] are in their turn of poorer quality than *their*[170] fathers and mothers, who no doubt had to face even[180] less easy conditions. Clearly, this cannot be the case, for[190] if we are today any better than the people[200] of a thousand or two thousand years ago, it is[210] because on the whole the young people at any given[220] time have been as good as the old people, and[230] even a little better. The material conditions of life for[240] the masses of the people of this country are better[250] today than they have ever been. People generally have[260] better food, better houses and better schools. More care is[270] taken to see that young people, as far as possible,[280] take up work of a kind which will interest them.[290] And almost all large business houses now provide playing fields[300] for their workers.

Not only are these better conditions offered[310] to the people—it is of equal importance to note[320] that the people are making full use of the better[330] conditions. Authorities all over the country have provided schools where[340] those who are at work during the day may increase[350] their knowledge in their free time, either without charge or[360] at a very low cost; and the attendances at such[370] schools are growing yearly. Women all over the country and[380] in every station of life are learning the food values[390] of different kinds of food, and people generally are moving[400] into the better kind of houses as soon as it[410] is possible for them to do so. More people own[420] their own houses today than at any time in[430] our history.

It is quite true that to learn to[440] face up to troubles and a hard life is a[450] valuable part of our training; but even though the material[460] conditions of our lives are better, we still have enough[470] troubles to face and to overcome in our own times[480] without wishing to turn our steps back into the past[490] in order to find still more.

That girls and young[500] women are today in a better position than their[510] mothers were would not be questioned by many. They can[520] lead very much wider and happier lives, and it is[530] certainly not the women who talk with love about the[540] good old days. But men have been doing it throughout[550] the years. Here is one example. An old man writes:[560]

"The minds of the young people are full of plays[570] and shows; and if they are so interested in these[580] things, what room is left over in their minds for[590] learning? And," he adds, "the teachers are just as bad.[600] With them, too, such subjects supply the material for talk[610] more often than any others."

We feel that we have[620] heard these words before. But when were they written? Nearly[630] two thousand years ago! Have we, after all, changed so[640] very much?   (642)

No. 36

We considered recently a few points regarding shorthand writing, and[10] it may be of interest if we now deal with[20] those points in a little more detail. You may remember[30] that our first point was that you, as shorthand writers,[40] should not regard *any* sort of paper as good enough[50] for shorthand notes. If the paper you use is of[60] poor quality you are making it less easy for yourself[70] in your attempts to write at a higher rate. Your[80] writing materials should *always* be of the very best quality,[90] both in your school work and at the office. Also,[100] you must train yourself to turn over a page very[110] quickly. Otherwise you will find that by the time you[120] have turned the page the reader will be too many[130] words in front of you. It has been found that[140] many shorthand writers fail to pass shorthand tests simply because[150] they have taken too long to turn over the page,[160] and so have lost several words. It is easy to[170] understand this when you consider that when you are writing[180] at the rate of 60 words a minute you are[190] writing one word a second; when you are writing at[200] 120 words a minute you are writing[210] two words a second. It is quite clear, therefore, that[220] you must not waste 5 or more of your valuable[230] seconds on turning over a page. It must be turned[240] without the waste of one second.

Our next point was[250] that the writer should develop a light and easy touch,[260] passing very quickly from one outline to the next and[270] from the end of one line to the beginning of[280] the next. We very often see shorthand writers, in the[290] early days of their training, writing much too heavily. Every[300] attempt should be made to overcome this, and it is[310] never too soon to begin. You can find out in[320] the following way whether you yourself are writing too heavily.[330] When you have written a page of shorthand turn to[340] the back of the page and see whether any marks[350] of your writing show through the paper. If they do,[360] you will know that you are not writing lightly enough[370] to get the best results. The notes of the good[380] shorthand writer can never be seen on the back of[390] the paper.

The third point was that you should have[400] a really good knowledge of the rules of the system[410] and of the special Short Forms, as you cannot hope[420] to build up a high rate of writing if you[430] do not know the rules of the system. The Short[440] Forms, by the way, represent a large part of any[450] matter which you are likely to be called upon to[460] take down in shorthand, and it will be of great[470] value to you if you can write them easily and[480] quickly, without trouble.

Read and copy well-written shorthand. In[490] this way you will form in your mind pictures of[500] the outlines for a great many words. When matter is[510] read out to you these pictures will come at once[520] to your mind and you will be able to put[530] the outlines on to paper without loss of time. If,[540] when taking down, there is a doubt in your mind[550] as to what is the right outline for a word,[560] write something which represents the sound of the word. Afterwards,[570] take steps to find out what the outline should be[580] and write it until you feel certain that you know[590] it and will in future be able to write it[600] quickly.

Finally, *never* let yourself think of other things while[610] you are taking shorthand notes. Think only of what you[620] are writing. At the end of a "take" you should[630] be able to give a short account of the subject[640] matter without looking at your notes. If you cannot do[650] this, it shows that you were not thinking of the[660] "sense" of the matter while you were writing. (668)

No. 37

The Englishman, it is widely believed, is always talking about[10] the weather. It is probably true that the people of[20] this country do talk about the weather more than is[30] the case in some other countries, but that is merely[40] because the English weather gives us more to talk about.[50] We simply do not know from one day to the[60] next what sort of weather we shall get, and sometimes[70] we really do not know from hour to hour. And[80] so it has become natural to us to talk about[90] the weather, and when we meet a friend we usually[100] make some such remark as: "What a lovely day!" or[110] perhaps: "What weather!" according to how we feel. Nor do[120] most of us like most of the weather. It is[130] either too warm or too cold; water comes down upon[140] us in such amounts that we feel like turning into[150] fishes, or it does not come at all and all[160] the plants we have so carefully put in the ground[170] are in danger of dying. No, we do not really[180] like our weather, but we are willing to state to[190] any who are willing to hear that our weather is[200] the best in the world. Far from us, we say,[210] is the desire for lovely warm days throughout the whole[220] of the year—and so on. The fact that we[230] state that our weather is the best in the world[240] does not, of course, mean that we have to like[250] it. And like it we do *not*, most of the[260] time. Perhaps that is why so many people go to[270] other countries for their two or three weeks' leave in[280] the summer. They are willing to put up with the[290] changing weather while they go about their day-to-day[300] working lives, but for those wonderful weeks when they are[310] free from work they want something better, some measure of[320] certainty that the days will be kind to them.

Yet,[330] when all is said and done, we know that there[340] is nothing quite like a lovely English summer day, a[350] summer day with warmth but without great heat—and that[360] is a very real difference —a summer day when the[370] evenings are long and we can sit outside or at[380] our windows and watch the beautiful golden and red colours[390] of the dying day. How peaceful are those sweet hours,[400] as we rest and talk, or read a little, or[410] tell ourselves once more "that the world is all right;[420] it is the people living in it that make it[430] seem all wrong!" Sweet indeed are such hours, and we[440] feel all the better for experiencing them.

And how lovely[450] are the first warm days towards the end of winter![460] There is nothing quite like the pleasure, after the hard[470] and cold days of winter, of getting up one morning[480] and finding a new warmth in the air, of seeing[490] the first signs of little leaves breaking through once again,[500] and feeling new life beginning all about us. Perhaps that[510] is why the English weather is said to be the[520] best in the world. Days such as these make so[530] deep a mark on our minds that we remember them[540] always. There are countries in the world whose advertisements state[550] that they have such days all the year round. But,[560] of course, that is not possible. Those first warm days[570] after winter when plant and animal life grows anew are[580] wonderful just because they are exceptional. They just could not[590] happen in the same form on every day of the[600] year and without the hard winter days coming first. Where[610] the weather never changes there can be no surprises, and[620] it is the surprise of those first warm days after[630] winter that is part of the pleasure.

Even days in[640] winter can be good. We do not mind feeling cold[650] when we are dressed for it. It is quite wonderful[660] to go for a long, quick walk on a winter's[670] day, when the ground under our feet is white and[680] hard and the air is so clear that we can[690] see for miles. Probably one of the biggest troubles about[700] the English weather is to be found not in the[710] weather itself but in ourselves. We just will not take[720] the weather seriously, and we just will not do the[730] things that would help to make us more comfortable. When[740] it is very, very cold and we find that our[750] supply of water is no longer waiting for us we[760] are quite surprised. We get out of bed and at[770] once we feel very, very cold. Of course, we ought[780] to have put in some form of heating throughout the[790] house years ago but—. Our windows let in the cold[800] air. We ought—. And that is the way it is[810] with us, the English.

Really, we just love our weather[820] and all that it does to us!   (827)

No. 38

From the ship the man was looking at the land[10] in the distance. He had been on the high seas[20] for nearly three months, and the ship had touched land[30] several times. Those land-falls had meant little to him,[40] however, because the only country he now had any desire[50] to see was the country ahead of him. At present[60] it was hardly more than a point showing above the[70] water. That country was home, his homeland that he had[80] left six years before.

His mind went quickly over those[90] six years of his life. He was a young man[100] of 24 when he had gone away. At 30[110] he believed himself to be quite old, and he certainly[120] looked more than his 30 years. On the other hand,[130] he looked the picture of health. Six years of trying[140] to make money in mines and on farms in the[150] far-off countries of the world had made him hard[160] and strong. Weather now had no personal meaning for him.[170] To be warm or to be cold was all the[180] same so far as his personal feelings went. Weather interested[190] him only through its influence on his work, whether he[200] was in the mines, in the building trade, or[210] on a farm. Weather influenced production and was, therefore, important; but[220] it did not influence him.

His face was quite heavily[230] lined for his years, the result of some of the[240] hard times he had experienced before finally making the big[250] money that he was looking for. He knew what it[260] was to be in the open through long cold nights,[270] and also what it was like to walk for mile[280] after mile in the burning heat. He knew what it[290] was like to go without food for several days at[300] a time, and he had experienced hours when he would[310] have given his whole future life for a simple drink[320] of water. He knew the value of water all right,[330] and he had made up his mind that, however long[340] he might live in the homeland, he would never touch[350] a hard drink.

Water had brought him back to life[360] when he was almost dying for want of it. He[370] would always remember the experience of opening his eyes to[380] see a man beside him and to feel the touch[390] of water at last. The man had had a horse,[400] and together they had reached the next town, weak though[410] he was. From that day on he had never drunk[420] anything but water or milk, and, he told

177

himself as[430] he continued to look at that point of land standing[440] up out of the water, he would not change his[450] mind when he reached there safely. Not one penny of[460] the hundreds of thousands of pounds that he now had[470] in the bank would be spent on hard drink, either[480] for himself or for his friends.

In his early days[490] he had several times nearly drunk himself out of this[500] world and into the next. The money he had laboured[510] so hard to get in the mines or on the[520] farms had been spent overnight, with not a penny[530] left to show for it. But things had changed after[540] he reached that town with the man on horseback who[550] had saved his life. They had become friends, and life[560] had taken on a new colour. The man was looking[570] for gold. He knew where to find it, he said,[580] but it was necessary for the two men to work[590] together. One man on his own could not take advantage[600] of the opportunities. To his great surprise his friend was[610] speaking the truth. They found the gold, and before a[620] year had passed they both had all the money that[630] anyone could desire.

Then the man on the ship remembered[640] something more. He had left a girl behind. Her eyes[650] were so wide open and blue when she looked at[660] him and said that she would wait that he had[670] complete trust in her words. Now he could not help[680] feeling doubtful. Would a girl wait for a man if[690] she heard nothing from him for six years? Common sense[700] said "No" but his heart said "Yes." (707)

(*Continued in No. 39*)

No. 39

(*Continued from No. 38*)

The girl was 18 years old when he went away.[10] There came before his eyes a memory of her so[20] clear that he was surprised. In all of his six[30] years he had never remembered her in that way. She[40] was as lovely as a summer morning, and she was[50] sweet and good. The waters of all the seas that[60] he had seen were not as blue as her eyes,[70] and no gold that he had mined was more beautiful[80] than the expression on her face when first he told[90] her that he loved her and asked her to wait[100] for him.

Being young, she was willing enough to wait[110] but she did not want him to go far away.[120] He would never return, she said. So many of the[130] old people she knew in that little town in the[140] Highlands had brothers or children who had gone away to[150] make money and who had never returned. Many of them[160] had never been heard of again.

He offered her comfort[170] for her fears, and said with his hand on his[180] heart that he would return to her. "I shall turn[190] up again, my love," he said, "like a bad penny.[200] But," he added, "I shall not come back with bad[210] pennies in my hand but with good gold in the[220] bank."

"Who said I wished for gold?" she cried, in[230] her fear. "A little farm in our lovely Highlands is[240] good enough for me."

But he made light of such[250] an idea. He told her that she was a girl[260] in a million, and he would make a million pounds[270] for her. When he was going away he made her[280] tell him once again that she would wait for him,[290] and then he stepped on to the ship, leaving her[300] crying.

As he thought of all these things he saw[310] that the land had become much clearer. Quite soon he[320] would be home. He had wired May as well as[330] his family, asking them to meet him. When he was[340] far away he had been full of certainty. His family[350] would be just as he had left them, and May[360] would not have changed. There she would be standing waiting[370] for him, her lovely face full of happiness. His old[380] mother, too, would be there, and his brother Will. But[390] all at once a real fear touched his heart. Why[400] should things be just the same at home when life[410] had changed so much for him? Why should he expect[420] them all to run to see him at the first[430] opportunity when he had left them almost without news for[440] so long? He found that he could not understand how[450] he went through all those years without writing to his[460] home more than two or three times. To May he[470] had never written. When he was doing badly and had[480] no money he did not wish to write and let[490] them know that he had had no success. When he[500] was successful and making money he had had no time[510] for writing letters. If no one was there to meet[520] him, what would he do?

He began to walk up[530] and down, up and down, trying to pass the hours[540] until the ship reached land. At last his ship was[550] within a mile of the homeland. The details of buildings[560] began to show up clearly, and quite quickly they were[570] very near. Then they were moving little by little, and[580] with a last movement the ship came to rest.

At[590] first he could see no one he knew. There were[600] others on the ship who also expected their families or[610] friends to meet them, and about a hundred people were[620] down there, looking up at the great ship and crying[630] out when they saw their dear ones on board.

179

Then[640] he saw five people standing on their own, away from[650] the others. An old man and woman, a young man[660] and a young woman, and a little boy of about[670] two years of age. He saw them clearly now, his[680] father and mother grown aged in those six years, and[690] his own May with his brother Will, each holding a[700] hand of the little boy. The truth came to him.[710] The girl really did want the simple life of the[720] Highlands! She had married his young brother, Will. (728)

No. 40

How old is old? How old are you and how[10] old is your father? Again how old is his father?[20] Maybe that last age seems very old to you who[30] are young. But are you young? What is the age[40] of the youngest baby in your family, either in your[50] own home or in the homes of your relations? Perhaps[60] the baby has lived for only a few months or[70] even a few hours, and you at sixteen years of[80] age must seem quite old to the baby's mother.

Age[90] is, indeed, anything but a simple thing. You cannot be[100] said to be young or old except in relation to[110] the age of some other person or thing. To the[120] young girl, starting life in the office for the first[130] time, her immediate chief may seem quite old. That chief[140] is probably, however, no more than 30 or 35[150] years of age, and he feels very young indeed when[160] he is with his Director, who is nearly 70. But[170] when the man who is nearly 70 sees the picture[180] in the newspaper of a happy old man or woman[190] who has reached one hundred years of age, he in[200] his turn feels young and almost boyish!

Again, everyone, whatever[210] his age may be, is so young as almost not[220] to have lived at all if his age is considered[230] side by side with that of the earth on which[240] he lives and has his being. The earth has been[250] in existence for millions of years, and the age of[260] mankind is as nothing if judged by the age of[270] the earth itself.

As we go through life we are[280] forced to the belief that too much importance is given[290] to a person's age. It is not the date on[300] a piece of paper that matters: it is the person's[310] state of health in body and mind. Some people are[320] quite old at 25 and others are still young[330] at 70. We might perhaps all be happier if less[340] importance were paid to age. Young people who express an[350] opinion are often told that they are "too young" to[360] know, and as a result very little attention is paid[370] to such expressions of opinion. Yet it is possible that[380] the young person has formed the opinion as a result[390] of reading, followed by careful thought, and he has every[400] right to his point of view. It is even possible[410] that the young person is at times right while the[420] person of more years is wrong. People do not always[430] get wiser as they increase in age: sometimes they do[440] and sometimes they do not. If it were not for[450] the new ideas of the younger people new developments might[460] often not take place.

Equally wrong, however, is it for[470] young people to make light of the opinions of their[480] fathers and mothers. Young people too often take no account[490] of the opinions of the old because it is so[500] easy to tell the old people that they are "out[510] of date." The father and mother of a young person[520] have lived longer and have had more experience.

This war[530] between the young and the old is not, we think,[540] in the least necessary. What is probably necessary is a[550] small change in outlook. In place of thinking of people's[560] ages we should think of them as being at different[570] parts of the road through life. If some people set[580] out for a walk at 8 in the morning, those[590] who set out for the same walk at 9 do[600] not regard those in front of them as being quite[610] out of the running and not worth consideration. Those who[620] set out an hour later still are quite willing to[630] regard the earlier walkers as being like themselves but as[640] having begun earlier and having therefore covered a little more[650] distance. Those who are in front look back to those[660] who are behind them, and perhaps feel some pleasure because[670] they have already covered more ground, but they respect the[680] others neither more nor less because they are in a[690] different position. We are all in different positions on the[700] road through life. Some of us began our walk on[710] the road early, and some set out a little later.[720] Some have hardly taken the first steps. We are all[730] on the same road together, and the distance we have[740] covered is of very little importance because we have all[750] to walk the road to the end of our lives,[760] even though the distances covered are not all quite the[770] same. Judged by the age of the earth the difference[780] in the number of years of our lives is as[790] nothing. (791)